THE JEANES TEACHER

Miss Anna T. Jeanes

THE JEANES TEACHER
IN THE UNITED STATES
1908-1933

AN ACCOUNT OF TWENTY-FIVE YEARS'
EXPERIENCE IN THE SUPERVISION OF
NEGRO RURAL SCHOOLS

By

LANCE G. E. JONES, M.A. (*Oxon.*), PH.D. (*Lond.*)

*Lecturer and Tutor in the Oxford University
Department of Education*

CHAPEL HILL
THE UNIVERSITY OF NORTH CAROLINA PRESS
1937

COPYRIGHT, 1937, BY
THE UNIVERSITY OF NORTH CAROLINA PRESS

TO
THE JEANES TEACHERS
OF THE
SOUTHERN STATES

Contents

	Preface	xi
CHAPTER		
I.	The Era of Opportunity	1
II.	Converging Paths	11
III.	Virginia Estelle Randolph: The First Jeanes Teacher	22
IV.	Early Days: Experiment and Expansion	39
V.	Progress by Co-operation	57
VI.	The Jeanes Teacher at Work	72
VII.	The Jeanes Work: Adaptation and Experiment	89
VIII.	After Twenty-Five Years	108
IX.	The Changing South	122
	Appendices	127
	Selected Bibliography	145

ILLUSTRATIONS

Miss Anna T. Jeanes	Frontispiece
	FACING PAGE
Map indicating route followed by author through the Southern States	8
Mr. Jackson Davis	14
Dr. James Hardy Dillard	18
Mr. B. C. Caldwell and Dr. Dillard	20
Dr. Dillard and Dr. Wallace Buttrick	20
Miss Virginia Randolph	24
Mountain Road School, 1911: Old Building renovated and enlarged	28
Mountain Road School: New Building, dedicated 1915	28
Gardening at Mountain Road School	32
Cooking class at Mountain Road School	32
Virginia Randolph County Training School: Jeanes Memorial Dormitory	36
Physical exercises at the Virginia Randolph County Training School	36
Virginia Randolph County Training School: New Building, 1930	40
Virginia Randolph at the entrance to the New Building of the County Training School	40

ILLUSTRATIONS

Home visits by Jeanes Teachers	44
Virginia Randolph visits a rural school	44
An unimproved rural home	50
An improved rural home	50
Dr. Dillard, Dr. W. T. B. Williams, and Mr. Jackson Davis	60
Mr. Jackson Davis and Dr. Dillard	60
A one-room rural school	64
A four-teacher consolidated school: Rosenwald Building	64
Mr. B. C. Caldwell with a class of rural ministers	70
Dr. Dillard confers with a Negro deacon at a preachers' institute	70
Two-teacher rural school in poor area: principal and a group of over-age pupils	74
A progressive teacher and her pupils	74
The Jeanes Teacher, 1934	80
The Jeanes Teacher visits a rural school, February, 1934	80
Assembling for a County Field Day	84
County Field Day: part of exhibit of industrial work	84
County Field Day: physical exercises	92
County Field Day: Maypole dancing	92
Exhibit of industrial work: chair caning	96
Exhibit of needlework	96
Assembling for a teachers' institute	100
A group of Jeanes Supervisors, 1917	100
A group of County Training School principals and Jeanes Teachers with officers of the Jeanes and Slater Funds, 1923	104
A group of Negro teachers	104

Preface

THE EARLY years of the twentieth century were the seedtime of many an educational enterprise in the southern part of the United States, and one of these forms the subject of this short study. Its beginnings were modest and inconspicuous; its initiators were men and women already alive to the South's great need. Thus in the autumn of 1905 the Negro teacher of a wayside school in Henrico County, Virginia, was striving with patience, tact, and resourcefulness to make her school a centre of community life; the Superintendent of Schools for the same county, a young Virginian, was bringing a quiet enthusiasm and sympathetic understanding to the support of every honest effort in education; while far away in New Orleans, another Virginian, dean of a Southern college, was entering into University and civic life with a zeal, sincerity, and zest for friendship which were rapidly carrying him forward into many a movement for the betterment of Southern life. None of them could have foretold that a few years later they would be co-operating to help the coloured people of their native state, or that the generosity of a little Quaker lady of

PREFACE

Philadelphia would make financially possible a movement in which each of them would play an important part. But so it was. In 1907 the Jeanes Fund was established and early in 1908 the college dean became its first president. Within the next few months the young County Superintendent was instrumental in directing the resources of the Fund into channels which were to determine the lines of future development, and the Negro teacher of the small wayside school became the first Jeanes Supervisor.[1] As later events were to show these three were pioneers in a co-operative effort which has sent out Supervisors in increasing numbers to help and encourage teachers in Negro rural schools, and which, by its success, has suggested similar enterprises in other lands.

The story of this development provides a fascinating record of human faith and achievement, to which I have tried to do justice. For much of the material on which my study is based I am indebted to those who have played a leading part in the events I record, and I have learned a great deal by personal observation and experience. Whenever necessary I have drawn also upon the printed papers and other records of the Jeanes Fund, as well as on various publications relating to Negro education. But the available materials are scattered, and I am not aware that there is in existence a concise and connected account of the work of the Jeanes Teachers

---

[1] The full title should be Jeanes Supervising Industrial Teacher, but more usually these teachers are referred to simply as Jeanes Supervisors or Jeanes Teachers.

PREFACE xiii

in each of its different aspects—social, educational, and historical. Such an account I have attempted to provide. I have not aimed at an exhaustive survey, lest by including overmuch material I should obscure the main outlines of my story. Primarily, too, I have in mind the reader who has no first hand knowledge of the conditions and activities which I describe, though I am not without hope that even those who have such knowledge may find an independent account of some interest.

My reasons for undertaking this study ought perhaps to be explained. Many years ago a comparison of English, and American education led me to consider the special problems of the Southern States, and in particular the situation which had arisen since 1865 as the result of a large and increasing Negro population. As a teacher I was naturally attracted by the schools for coloured people, and in the spring of 1927, a timely grant from Oxford University enabled me to spend a period of four months studying these schools at close quarters. Once in the South, Negro rural schools and their problems aroused my interest, and the report which I then prepared included a chapter on "The Supervision of Rural Schools," a subject which I could see would merit fuller exploration.[2] The opportunity for this came when, in the spring of 1934, a generous grant from the Carnegie Corporation of New York made it possible for me to spend a further period of four months in the Southern States, and continue my investi-

[2] The report was published in 1928 by the Oxford University Press under the title, *Negro Schools in the Southern States*.

gations.[3] To the Carnegie Corporation, to my University colleagues who made absence from Oxford possible, and to the Oxford University Delegates for the Training of Teachers, who readily granted me the necessary leave, I wish to express my very sincere thanks.

I have had many willing helpers and am deeply grateful to them all—the officers of the Carnegie Corporation, the General Education Board, and the Phelps-Stokes Fund, the past and present officers of the Jeanes Fund, State Agents for Negro schools, principals of Negro schools which I have visited and with whom I have conferred, and last, but by no means least, the many Jeanes Teachers I have met, and who have talked with me freely of their work. I have met them in all kinds of places—on the road, in the office, in the schools—often singly, sometimes in pairs, or again in larger groups. We have met by appointment, we have met by chance, and always they have courteously and generously shared with me their experience. If I have understood their problems aright it is because of the freedom of our discussions; if I have conveyed to the reader anything of their spirit it is from them that I have caught it; and as a token of my appreciation of their help, and a tribute to their faithful service in the cause of education I gladly dedicate this small volume to them.

For many of the illustrations, including the portrait of Miss Virginia Randolph, I am indebted to Mr. Jackson Davis, who has generously allowed me to draw

[3] The map facing page 8 shows the ground covered in my two journeys through the South.

PREFACE

upon his excellent collection of photographs. The photographs of Mr. Jackson Davis and Dr. Dillard are included by permission of these gentlemen. The portrait of Miss Anna T. Jeanes is reproduced by the kind permission of Mr. Arthur D. Wright, President of the Board of Trustees of the Jeanes Fund. The remaining illustrations are from photographs taken either by myself or by State Agents with whom I visited schools.

That I should have ventured once again to commit my observations and conclusions to writing is in part due to those American friends of both races, who by their appreciation of my earlier survey encouraged me to complete this supplementary study. But for the form which it takes, for any expression of opinion which it contains, and for whatever sins of omission and commission the reader may detect, I alone am responsible. I am conscious, for example, that I have only sketched in very lightly the larger social issues which form the background to my study; I am well aware, too, that by concentrating on one phase of educational development I may seem to have exaggerated its importance. Such limitations and such apparent exaggerations are inevitable, and the reader will be able to make his own allowances. But when every allowance has been made I trust that no one will be left in doubt as to the significance of this movement in the educational and social history of the South. Not only has it covered the countryside with Jeanes Teachers and brought help and hope to many a rural school, but in times both of prosperity and adversity it has provided a channel through which the better elements of both races have been able to find expression in co-operative effort for the common good. Only by such common effort can the more generous social traditions of the South be preserved, and handed on as a still worthier inheritance to future generations.

LANCE G. E. JONES

Oxford
January, 1936

THE JEANES TEACHER

I

THE ERA OF OPPORTUNITY

"NOT FOR an hour has the South been conscious of peace. The sense of uneasiness has been perennial." [1] In these vivid words, written forty years after the last Confederate soldier had laid down his arms, a Southerner lays bare the tragedy of the peace that was no peace, the shadow that darkened the years which followed the Civil War. Desolation and destitution, mistrust and fear, were everywhere to be found, and the errors and inefficiency of so-called Reconstruction governments did but add fuel to the smouldering fires of discontent in every Southern State. By 1880 these governments had passed: the Southern white man was again in control, and another phase in the history of the South had begun. It proved, alas, to be one of the South's "dark ages," and bequeathed a heavy legacy to future generations—a South politically solid and for the most part politically dead, an economy increasingly dependent on the fortunes of a single crop, tenant

[1] Edgar Gardner Murphy, *The Basis of Ascendancy*, p. 190.

farmers tied by share-cropping and peonage,[2] private schools and colleges isolated from the main stream of life and thought, public schools insufficient in number and poor in quality, and a steadily increasing coloured population cut off from almost every avenue to social and economic advancement. At times it seemed as though the current of Southern life had ceased to flow. Men looked backward not forward, their heroes were Confederate veterans, their "golden age" the days of the Old South.

In some ways and for some folk it had been a land of beauty, charm, and comfort, and writers from Thomas Nelson Page onwards have not ceased to sing its praises. By contrast the New South was a land of poverty, desolation and unrest, and the new age an age of despair. Fortunately, there were those to whom the grim desolateness of the times was a challenge, and whose faith in their homeland enabled them to see it as a land of opportunity. Some, like the Confederate general, Robert E. Lee, who became head of a Southern college, strove earnestly for "the allayment of passion, the dissipation of prejudice and the restoration of reason," for the unity without which no true recovery was possible. Others, such as Henry Grady, preached the revival and development of industry, while still others, with Sidney Lanier, looked for a return to the small farm with a new and richer life arising, as he said, out of the ground.

---

[2] Under a share-cropping system an agreed proportion of the crop, usually one half, goes to the landlord. Peonage was virtually involuntary servitude, with the obligation to discharge debt by labour.

ERA OF OPPORTUNITY

Foremost of all in advocating forward policies in every sphere of life was Walter Hines Page, whose address at Greensboro, North Carolina, in 1897, on "The Forgotten Man" roused the Southerner from his apathy, and impelled him either to aid or to resist the new currents of life that were beginning to flow. Page proclaimed the South's industrial awakening as the most important economic event in American history since the settlement of the West, constituted himself the champion of every movement designed to better the condition of the people, and until he became Ambassador to the Court of St. James and left for England in 1913, never ceased his efforts to extend and improve public education in the Southern States. With Lee he desired "the thorough education of all classes," but most of all was he concerned for those who until then had been "isolated, side-tracked, kept back from the highways of life," the South's forgotten men and women.[3]

More and more as the nineteenth century drew to a close men's minds turned towards the schools, and to education as the South's great need and hope. There had been public schools for white folk before the war, but they fell into disuse when the reforming zeal of Reconstruction governments threw them open also to the Negro. Fortunately, from 1867 onwards the influence of the Peabody Fund, the wisdom of its Board of Trustees,

---

[3] Burton J. Hendrick, *The Life and Letters of Walter H. Page*. Vol. I, Chap. III, "The Forgotten Man," gives a vivid account of Page's activities at this time. From 1908 to 1919 Page was a very interested and active member of the Board of Trustees of the Jeanes Fund, and his son is now (1936) Chairman of that Board.

and the zeal and understanding of its general agents kept alive and fostered many a humble educational enterprise, and when opportunity offered no one preached more effectively the cause of the public schools than its second general agent, J. L. M. Curry. Before city councils, county courts, state legislatures, and committees of Congress, he pleaded with eloquence and effect. His example and enthusiasm inspired others to work for the same cause, and by 1900 their efforts were beginning to bear fruit.[4]

The Peabody Fund is of importance, too, in another way. By entrusting large sums of money to a Board of Trustees to be administered "for the welfare of the suffering South," George Peabody, the successful business man with unlimited faith in his country and in education, was setting an example which was destined to bring a new and valuable influence into Southern education. In 1882, seeing the benefits which had accrued to the South from the wise administration of the Peabody Fund, John F. Slater of Norwich, Connecticut, committed to a Board of Trustees the sum of one million dollars "for the furthering of Negro education," and in 1903 the incorporation of the General Education Board to administer the gifts of John D. Rockefeller brought into the field still another agency which, because its purpose was to promote education within the United States of America without distinction of race, sex, or creed, was later to prove of very great assistance

[4] An interesting account of the pioneers of this period will be found in Edwin Mims, *The Advancing South*, Chaps. I-III.

ERA OF OPPORTUNITY 5

to Southern schools for both white and coloured people. Finally, in line with the same tradition of philanthropy, was the establishment, in 1907, of the Jeanes Fund, of which we shall have more to say in a later chapter.

The welcome financial aid which these Trust Funds made available was but one of the benefits they conferred on Southern schools. Their administration and distribution brought able men from both North and South into frequent personal contact, and they, in their turn, did much to promote an enlightened and sympathetic understanding of the South's educational problems. In this few were more successful than Robert C. Ogden, a New York merchant, who in 1900, three years after Page's Greensboro address, presided over a small group of men meeting for the third successive year at Capon Springs, West Virginia, to consider the situation in the South. Out of these meetings grew the Conference for Education in the South, which one writer describes as "an annual meeting for advertising the educational needs of the South," and finally, a more permanent organization was set up known as the Southern Education Board, which paved the way for many later developments.[5] Robert Ogden and his friends had been building better than they knew, for, as Walter Page said graphically, "If Ogden had known more about 'Education' or more about 'the South, by gawd, Sir!' he'd never have

[5] An account of these meetings and conferences is given in Edgar Gardner Murphy, *The Present South*, Chap. VII. The same chapter also gives details of the early activities of the Southern Education Board and of the General Education Board. See also *The General Education Board; An Account of Its Activities, 1902-1914*, Chap. I.

had the courage to tackle the job." But, adds Page, "He turned out to be the wisest man on that task in our generation. He united every real good force, and showed what can be done in a democracy even by one zealous man." [6] The influence of Ogden's "public spirited excursions" was destined to be very far-reaching. Men's eyes were being opened, their minds roused from apathy and indifference. The widening of their horizons had begun.

Meantime, what of the Negro? Emancipated and subsequently enfranchised, but having neither knowledge nor experience of public affairs, he welcomed the aid of those who called themselves friends, and fell an easy prey to the "carpetbaggers" whose brief period of influence completed the economic ruin of the South. With equal eagerness but less disastrous consequences he flocked to those other and truer friends who came South to establish schools in the hope of fitting him for his new responsibilities. Some devoted their energies to the setting up of primary schools, high schools, and liberal arts colleges, of a type with which they were already familiar: others, and Samuel Chapman Armstrong in particular, preferred a less conventional approach. Placed in charge of Tidewater Virginia by the Freedmen's Bureau, Armstrong established the school now known the world over as Hampton Institute, and endeavoured, as he said, "to educate the whole man," [7] to

---

[6] Hendrick, *op. cit.* I, 126.
[7] Francis G. Peabody, ed., *Education for Life: The Story of Hampton Institute*, p. 29; "Educate the whole man is the idea; fit the pupil for the life he is likely to lead."

ERA OF OPPORTUNITY 7

teach the Negro to work with his hands, to use his mind in his work, and with his heart to love and serve God and his fellow men. Slowly the influence of these schools permeated the South, and when Booker T. Washington, the Negro principal of Tuskegee Institute in Alabama, pleaded in a speech at Atlanta in 1895 for co-operation between the races,[8] he was speaking for a race which had already proved its worth. In some places his message, like the seed in the parable, fell on good ground and brought forth much fruit; elsewhere the ground was stony and the seed was choked. The South heard, but the South was divided.

Many were genuinely afraid. Might not the rise of an educated and self-supporting Negro population forebode a renewal of the tragic happenings of Reconstruction days, and would not the training of Negroes to undertake skilled work threaten the economic security of the white worker? And because fear is contagious, and is the strongest and most inhibiting of human emotions, the liberal elements in Southern life and thought seemed to fade away, and the Negro was called upon once again to pass through "the valley of the shadow." The State of Mississippi led the way in 1890 by amending its franchise laws so as to make legally possible the exclusion of the coloured voter; South Carolina, Louisiana, North Carolina, Alabama, Virginia, Georgia, and Oklahoma followed suit, and by 1910 the

---

[8] "In all things that are purely social we can be as separate as the fingers, yet one as the hand in all things essential to mutual progress." For the whole address see Booker T. Washington, *Up From Slavery: An Autobiography*, Chap. XIV.

Negro's political freedom had virtually ceased to exist in most of the Southern States. Disfranchisement, too, was the prelude to repression amounting at times to persecution. Thus in 1892, and also in 1893, the number of Negro lynchings reached the unprecedented total of 155, and although such a figure was never again recorded, the number for the twenty-year period, 1890 to 1910, exceeded 2,000. Such figures need no elaboration.[9]

Yet now, as ever, the South held men with larger hearts, wider vision, and a deeper sense of justice. Governor Aycock defending before a critical legislature his attempts to help the neglected Negro schools of North Carolina, George Foster Peabody lending his support to the young principal of a struggling Negro school in Georgia—these and others of like mind and courage were determined not to lose hope. The futility and degradation of a policy dictated by fear became more and more evident: thoughtful men and women in every state began to listen, with interest if not with approval, to the appeal of those who, like Edgar Gardner Murphy, were stirred to public utterance by the tragedy of Southern ignorance and poverty.

There was little that was new in his message: what was significant was that a Southerner by birth and upbringing should feel impelled not merely to discuss ways and means of dealing with present problems, but to go further and lay bare the ultimate issues in South-

---

[9] *The Negro Year Book, 1931-32*, p. 293. It is important also to note that in 1892 no less than 100 lynchings of white persons are recorded, and for the twenty years 1890-1910 the number of whites lynched was 626. These figures are indicative of the lawlessness then prevalent.

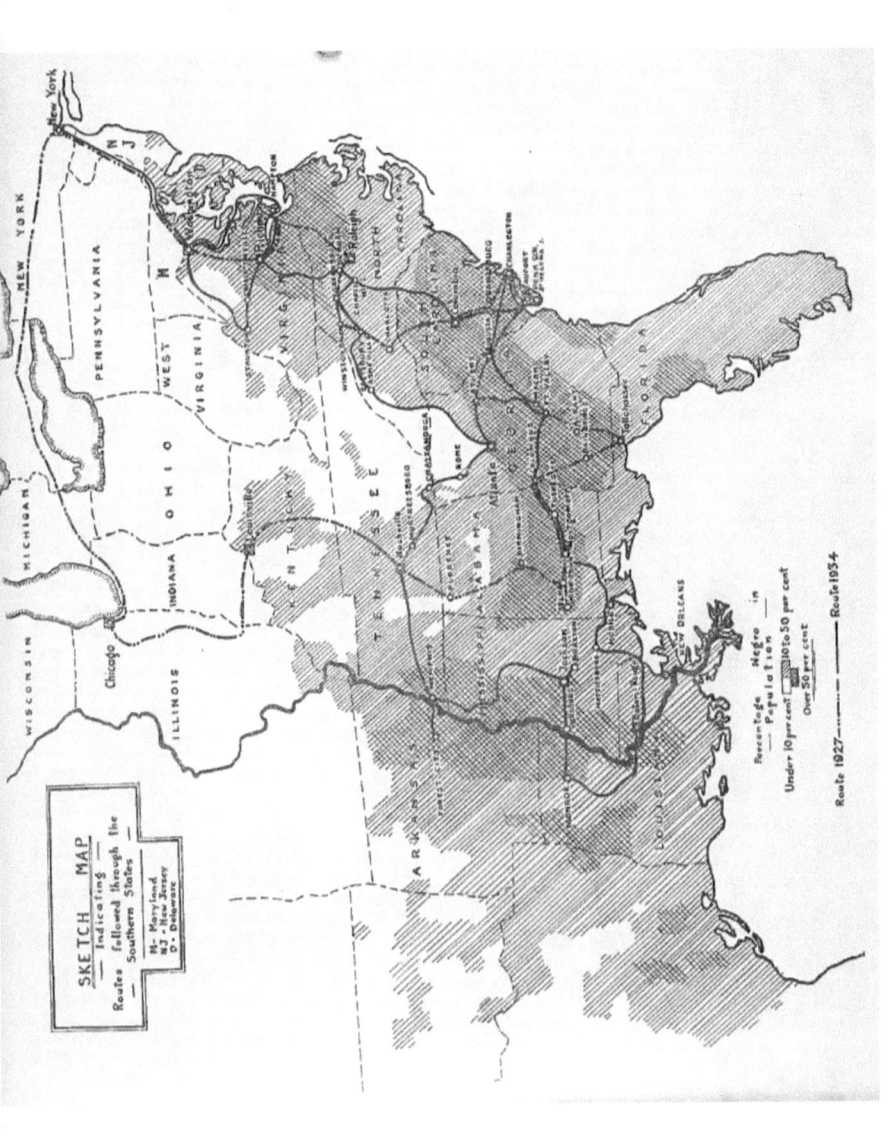

ern life in order to seek a rational basis for their solution—should discuss not merely "The Present South," but also "The Basis of Ascendancy." [10] He deplored Southern antagonisms and Southern illiteracy, criticised Southern industry for its use of child labour, and Southern schools for their backwardness, praised where he could and blamed where he felt he must, while all the time with increasing insistence he stressed the larger issues of race and of democracy. He knew well that for the South every social and economic problem was also a Negro problem, and refused to consider any solution which failed to take this into account. He deplored the closed mind of the South on all questions relating to the Negro, and pointed out that by their attitude Southerners were denying the very principles of democracy which they professed, and curtailing even their own freedom. To quote his own words:

> The fundamental issue is not what we will do with the Negro, but what we will do with our institutions. In so far as we shall choose as the forms of our own free self-determination those and only those which involve the free self-determination of our included groups, the free activity of each must advance and fulfil our own. No true freedom can retard our freedom ... the birthright of every genuine social factor is not "immunity" but the tonic power of the fair chance,—is not "privilege" but democracy.[11]

The new life which was flowing through the veins of the South, Murphy insisted, was a challenge to

---
[10] These are the titles of his best known published works.
[11] Murphy, *The Basis of Ascendancy*, pp. 198-200.

service, but zeal must be tempered by knowledge, and by a clear grasp of the issues involved. He pointed out, for example, that races are undoubtedly different and racial integrity was therefore essential: that the problems of the South were certainly not the same as the problems of the North, but that the nation was one, and co-operative effort should be welcomed. Above all he emphasised the devitalizing and degrading influence of any policy of social improvement which failed also to improve the South's Negro population—both races must come forward together. Finally, like many of his contemporaries, he urged that "it is to the school—the school in its every form, from the rural 'primary' to the university, that our democracy must look, and may look, for the more satisfactory adjustment of the problems which accompany and affect its progress." [12]

It was in times such as these, when men and women in the Southern States were becoming increasingly conscious both of the great need of their people and of new opportunities for service, that the Jeanes Teachers began their work.

[12] Murphy, *The Present South*, p. 285.

II

Converging Paths

IN VIRGINIA, oldest and in some ways most conservative of the Southern States, the educational revival did not take effect until after 1902. A new state constitution adopted in that year made possible a closer supervision of schools, and in 1904 Governor Montague summoned a conference of men and women prominent in the state to discuss problems of rural life and education. Out of this conference was formed a Co-operative Education Commission; this in turn organized three larger and more representative conferences, planned and carried through, in May, 1905, a great campaign for the awakening of rural life and the improvement of rural schools, and finally, towards the end of the same year, took permanent shape as the Co-operative Education Association of Virginia. Thereafter, under the stimulus and guidance of "The Co-operative," local committees sprang up in every part of the state, and men and women worked together in these committees with such success that eighteen years later the editor of the Richmond *News-Leader* declared that "to attempt to list the services the Association has performed would be

THE JEANES TEACHER

to catalogue much of Virginia's progress in the last decade."[1] Some of those who co-operated to bring about this desirable result were particularly interested in the Negro, and two of them, Hollis Burke Frissell and Jackson Davis, were directly concerned in the events leading to the appointment of the first Jeanes Teacher.

Hollis Burke Frissell succeeded General Armstrong as Principal of Hampton Institute in 1893, and participated eagerly in the events described above. His judgment of men enabled him to see the ability of J. D. Eggleston, Jr., who had been elected State Superintendent of Schools in 1905, and to support him wholeheartedly; his wise counsel and the fertility of his mind made him the directing influence in the formation and subsequent activities of the Co-operative Education Association; and his devotion to the cause of the Negro was a guarantee that in the general enthusiasm for social improvement the coloured people of the state would not be forgotten.

No man brought more light to the forgotten people of the state, black and white. He asserted this influence not through any position he held but through his personality. In fact no important conference of educational leaders of the state was ever held that did not seek his presence and his wise counsel. He gave light and hope and cheer wherever he went. There was something in his quiet manner which spoke far more eloquently than any words he uttered. One remembered his faith

[1] Quoted in a pamphlet issued by the Co-operative Educational Association of Virginia in 1926, reviewing the progress of the movement.

and sympathy, and felt a keener sense of responsibility after a visit with him.[2]

Jackson Davis, who pays this high tribute to Dr. Frissell, first met him at the Lynchburg Conference of the Co-operative Education Commission. At that time Davis was Superintendent of Schools for Henrico County, a post to which the State Board of Education had appointed him on the recommendation of State Superintendent Eggleston, whose magnetic personality was already attracting able young men into the public service. This was not Jackson Davis's first experience of schools, for, after graduating from the College of William and Mary in 1902, he taught for two years in high school. His new duties, however, greatly enlarged his experience; they took him into the public schools for both white and coloured people, and gave him a clearer understanding of their needs. At the Lynchburg Conference he was called upon to read a report on the schools of his county, and when he sat down Dr. Frissell took him by the hand. He had recognised in the young Superintendent of Schools a kindred spirit.

Like many others of his generation Jackson Davis had followed with interest the writings and speeches of men like Walter Hines Page, and in particular had been attracted by the social and economic interpretation of Southern life put forward by Clarence H. Poe, with its emphasis on rural life, and on the self-support-

[2] From manuscript copy of an article by Jackson Davis on "The Influence of Dr. Frissell upon the Rural Schools of Virginia."

ing household as the basis of a healthy, happy society. More than usually sensitive to what he saw around him, Davis quickly became aware of the poverty and ignorance of the great mass of the people, and of the Negro in particular, and when in 1909 he was appointed a member of the State Board of Examiners, his experience of educational and social problems was still further enlarged. The Board issued all teachers' licences within the state, and each of its four members was responsible for a district of about twenty-five counties, within which he was expected to stimulate local effort, to see what local taxes could be raised to supplement state grants, and to push forward the provision of high schools for white pupils. While so engaged, Davis's interest in the economic and social problems of the state and of the South deepened, and he was seriously thinking of taking up college teaching in order to study these problems more closely, when an unexpected sequence of events led to his appointment in May, 1910, as the first State Agent for Negro Schools. But this is to anticipate our story.

Hampton Institute in Tidewater Virginia is only eighty-six miles from Richmond, the capital city of Virginia and the headquarters for Henrico County, and it was natural that Jackson Davis should visit the school. There he saw for himself the practical way in which Hampton was educating the Negro to become a useful and honourable member of the community, and when in the course of official visits to schools as County Superintendent he came to Mountain Road School, a

Mr. Jackson Davis

little one-room school in Henrico County which had been transformed by its teacher into a hive of activity and a centre of community life, he recognized the application of the same principles in an even humbler sphere, and determined to encourage the teacher in her good work. Her name was Virginia Randolph, and as Jackson Davis has told us of his early visits to the school he shall speak for himself.

Twenty years ago I came to this county as superintendent of schools. I remember coming to the closing exercises of this school the first year with Mr. and Mrs. John Stewart Bryan. The school was held in the old building you see on the other side. The old building was whitewashed and made attractive with vines and flowers. The yard was neat and orderly. The exercises were held out of doors. In the midst of one of the numbers we were somewhat startled by a fusillade of pistol shots a short distance down the road. The next break in the program the principal was on her feet saying that those shots were not fired by the people of this neighborhood. They did not do things like that. There were some strange people in a nearby camp, working on the Ashland Railway then under construction.

The splendid way in which she was serving this community so that she was identified with it and spoke for it made a lasting impression upon me. Though her home was in the city, she came back every Sunday afternoon and conducted Sunday School.

The next event that stands out in my mind was a Kitchen Opening. I had never heard of one before. The teachers had raised money and bought a cook stove. They and the pupils invited their friends to come and bring a utensil. In this way they began their cooking lessons.

Here was a teacher who thought of her work in terms of the welfare of the whole community, and of the school as an agency to help the people to live better, to do their work with more skill and intelligence and to do it in the spirit of neighborliness.[3]

With Jackson Davis to see a good thing was to wish to extend its benefits to others. By his visits to Hampton and his conversations with Dr. Frissell he had become familiar with the extension method of school improvement. Teachers were going out from Hampton to help the small rural schools, and this work had been facilitated by gifts of money from a Miss Anna T. Jeanes of Philadelphia. Could not some such scheme be devised to help the small rural schools of Henrico County by spreading the ideas and methods of Virginia Randolph? This was the question which at once arose in the mind of Jackson Davis. Dr. Frissell was sympathetic and suggested that Davis should write to a gentleman named Dr. Dillard who, with himself and Dr. Samuel Mitchell,[4] was co-trustee of a Fund recently established by Miss Jeanes to help the small Negro schools. The Fund was that which we now know as the Jeanes Fund, and we

---

[3] Address by Jackson Davis at the dedication of a new dormitory at the Henrico County Training School, Virginia, Nov. 18, 1924 (manuscript copy).

[4] Dr. S. C. Mitchell was one of the leaders of the educational revival in Virginia, and has been associated with most of the progressive movements in Southern education. He was one of the original Trustees of the Jeanes Fund, and has served continuously on the Jeanes Board down to the present time.

CONVERGING PATHS

must pause for a moment to consider its origin and purpose.

In 1904 Miss Anna T. Jeanes, a Quaker lady of Philadelphia, decided to take up residence in a home which she had built and endowed for the use of aged and infirm members of the Philadelphia Quarterly Meeting of the Society of Friends. Here she lived in quiet retirement until her death in 1907, and here in 1904 Dr. Frissell found her, when, on the advice of George Foster Peabody, he sought her help for Hampton Institute. Her answer to his request was unexpected. "Yes," she said, "I know all about Hampton, and I won't give any money to that. But I want to hear about the poor little Negro cabin one-teacher rural schools. Can thee tell me about these schools? I want to know about them." Dr. Frissell was pleased to comply with her wishes, and when at the end of the interview she handed him a cheque for $10,000 he was taken completely by surprise. The money was to enable Hampton to help the small rural schools near by; and soon afterwards when Booker T. Washington, of Tuskegee, called to see Miss Jeanes, he too was gladdened by the gift of a similar cheque for the same purpose. It was this timely help that enabled Hampton to undertake the extension work which had attracted the attention of Jackson Davis.

But the little lady's benefactions did not end here. George Foster Peabody, at that time Treasurer of the General Education Board, was able so to interest her in the activities of the Board on behalf of

Negro schools that in April, 1905, she entrusted to it a sum of $200,000, the income from which the Board still administers. But the final proof of her interest in Negro education came when, in 1907, she determined to set aside a sum of no less than $1,000,000 "for the furthering and fostering of rudimentary education" in small Negro rural schools, stipulating that William Howard Taft, Andrew Carnegie, Hollis Burke Frissell, Booker T. Washington, and George Foster Peabody should be members of the first Board of Trustees. The necessary formalities were duly completed, and the deed of trust signed by Miss Jeanes on the 22nd of April, 1907. The certificate of incorporation was dated November 20th, 1907, and the first regular meeting of the Incorporation of the Negro Rural School Fund was held in New York on the 29th of February, 1908.[5]

These, in bare outline, are the events which led to the establishment of the Jeanes Fund, and with a directness which matched her generosity Miss Jeanes laid down the purpose for which the money was to be used. She wished the Fund to be known as "The Fund for Rudimentary Schools for Southern Negroes," and the income to be devoted

to the one purpose of assisting, in the Southern United States, Community, Country, or Rural Schools for that great class of Negroes to whom the small Rural and Community Schools are alone available.[6] Furthermore,

[5] Arthur D. Wright, ed., *The Negro Rural School Fund, Inc.* (Anna T. Jeanes Foundation). *See* pp. 1-10 for a fuller account both of Miss Jeanes and of the establishment of the Jeanes Fund.
[6] *Ibid.*, p. iii. Extract from Miss Jeanes's will.

Dr. James Hardy Dillard

CONVERGING PATHS

as though these instructions were not sufficiently clear, Miss Jeanes directed that the Endowment Fund should be devoted

solely to the assistance of Rural, Community, or Country Schools for *Southern* Negroes, and not for the benefit or use of large institutions, *but for the purpose of rudimentary education* and to encourage moral influence and social refinement which shall promote peace in the land, and good will among men.[7]

Not all benefactors are so clear as to their intentions. That Miss Jeanes knew her own mind was illustrated also by an incident which occurred a few months before she died. She had insisted on the investment of her gift in government securities of certain kinds, and the Trustees asked that more latitude as to investment might be allowed. However, Miss Jeanes refused, and subsequent events have demonstrated that her refusal was justified.[8]

The first business of the Trustees was to elect officers, and in particular to choose a president who, as chief executive officer, would be responsible for the detailed administration of the Fund. Their choice fell upon James Hardy Dillard, Professor of Latin in Tulane University, New Orleans, and his appointment brought into the Jeanes work one who for more than twenty-three years was its guiding genius, and whose

[7] *Ibid.* The words in italics were inserted by Miss Jeanes into the draft copy of the will.
[8] Wright, *op. cit.*, p. 10.

name will always be inseparably associated with its early history.[9]

"Doctor Dillard of the Jeanes Fund," as his biographer calls him,[10] was fifty-one years of age when he began Jeanes work. To it he brought a personal knowledge of almost every phase of Southern life, a mind ripened by a sound classical education and later studies in law, as well as the experience gained by ten years' service as a teacher in schools, and twenty as teacher and administrator in Southern universities. Since 1891 he had been Professor of Latin at Tulane University, and since 1894 Dean of the College of Arts and Sciences. His activities and interests outside the College were too varied and extensive to enumerate here; it is worth noting, however, that they reveal a steadily growing interest in the Negro. He saw to it that one branch of the new Carnegie Library in New Orleans was for Negroes, he became trustee of four Southern Negro colleges, he heard of and approved the work of Armstrong at Hampton, of Booker Washington at Tuskegee, and of other teachers, white and coloured, who were struggling against heavy odds to maintain and develop their schools. He knew and was known by most of the men of light and leading in the South, and when in 1907, at the instance of Dr. Wallace Buttrick of the

---

[9] For twenty-two years Dr. Dillard was ably assisted in the Jeanes work by B. C. Caldwell of Louisiana, who acted as Field Director. The Minutes of the Jeanes Trustees for the meeting of April 28, 1932, record Mr. Caldwell's "faithful capable service" and acknowledge the debt of the Board to him "for so ably translating into action its purposes and ideals." *Ibid.*, p. 152.

[10] Benjamin Brawley, *Doctor Dillard of the Jeanes Fund.*

Mr. B. C. Caldwell and Dr. Dillard

Dr. Dillard and Dr. Wallace Buttrick

General Education Board, Dillard attended an informal meeting of the Trustees of the Jeanes Foundation, he was unanimously elected president. At first he refused the appointment; love for his work as a teacher and the modesty which is part of his charm, made him disinclined to undertake this new responsibility, and it needed the persuasions of his friends to overcome his hesitation.[11] He entered upon his new duties at the beginning of 1908, and was formally elected president at the first regular meeting of the Trustees in February of the same year.[12] It was to Dr. Dillard, in his capacity as President of the Jeanes Fund, that Jackson Davis's request for help came. From such a man it was assured of a sympathetic reception, and the correspondence which ensued was the beginning of a friendly co-operation which has continued without a break to the present time.

[11] The argument used by one of these friends, a leading banker in New Orleans, is worth noting. "We Southern people must realise our obligation, and if they are willing to entrust the expenditure of that money to you, it is your duty to do it." For Dillard's account of this incident see his address at the Conference on "What White People Can Do to Promote Negro Education," held at George Peabody College for Teachers, July, 1930.
[12] Wright, *op. cit.*, p. 33.

III

Virginia Estelle Randolph
The First Jeanes Teacher

I FIRST MET Virginia Randolph in February, 1927, when in company with Mr. Cooper, the County Superintendent of Schools, I paid my first visit to the Henrico County Training School. It was in the morning, shortly before the mid-day recess, and in the school kitchen quietly directing the girls at their tasks I found Miss Randolph, the Jeanes Supervisor for the county. It so happened that she was the first Jeanes Teacher I had met, and what I saw and heard that day made me anxious to know more, not only about Virginia Randolph, but about the work which she and hundreds of other Jeanes Teachers were doing for Negro rural schools. I have met her on several occasions since then, have heard her describe to others her many activities and her difficulties, and have talked with her at length about them. With her help and the help of my Southern friends I have set in order some of the things I have learnt about her.

The record may fitly begin with an account in her

VIRGINIA ESTELLE RANDOLPH

own words of her early life and education to the age of eighteen years, when she was appointed teacher of the school in which I met her, the school at the time of her appointment being only a typical one-room rural school.

I was born in Richmond, Virginia, June 8, 1874, next to the oldest of four children. My father died when my youngest sister was one month old, leaving my mother with four children. She had to pay rent for one room, and it was quite a task to take care of us, but she worked night and day, and it was due to the support from my mother's white friends that we made out.

My mother was born a slave and being very apt in household duties, spent most of her time sewing, but when the cook was out of place, she fitted nicely in the kitchen. Her people lived a long time after the war, her master being one of the Professors at the old Richmond College, now the University of Richmond. She was born in Campbell county. Her maiden name was Sarah Elizabeth Carter. Her white people witnessed her marriage to Edward Nelson Randolph, and had the pleasure of naming the four children.

I entered Baker School in Richmond, at six years of age, with Miss Virginia Bowen as my teacher. I could not learn my alphabet. After giving the teacher so much trouble in trying to have me repeat them I was started off reading, and at the end of the term received a medal for highest honour. At eight years of age I began working for Mrs. Powell, just two blocks from where I am now living, going to school and working mornings and evenings. I am proud to say that I am now living in the next block to where I was born and some of the white people that knew me from childhood are yet living in the neighborhood. My mother worked out three days in the week and then had five families' washing at home. She would wash and iron some nights all night in order to keep the four children in school. The wood yard then used to be at Munford and Broad streets, and Mr. Ford, the manager, knowing how my mother was struggling, would allow us to get chips to help with the fire. We only had one room, but that was kept clean, for my mother's motto was: "Cleanliness is next to Godliness."

The first Monday in every month was my mother's day to visit the school to find out just what we were doing. We lived about ten blocks from Baker School. She gave us fifteen minutes to get home and when I went to the old Normal, which was twice as far, she gave me thirty minutes. I remember having an Algebra teacher, by the name of Miss Henrietta Bass. If she heard the least noise, she would close the Algebra and have the lesson after three P.M. I would cry because I knew that meant a whipping for me, because my mother would think I was disobedient. After getting about a dozen whippings, I asked a child whom my mother had confidence in to tell my mother just what Miss Bass would do, and then she spared me a little.

I was reared from birth in Second Baptist Church. My mother would give us a buttered roll apiece, and send us to Sunday School. We had to stay to morning service and had our breakfast and dinner when we got back. Very often the dresses we wore all the week were washed and ironed on Saturday to wear to Sunday School. We often went bare-footed. Our dresses were given by the white people and my mother taught us to sew. She would cut them over and sometimes get two dresses out of one. I was taught to knit, sew, and crochet

Miss Virginia Randolph

by my mother, and my stockings, gloves, and all laces worn were homemade. I always had nice handkerchiefs, as my mother would save flour bags. School handkerchiefs were made with half a flour bag. Sunday ones were made with the bag cut in fourths. Those bags were nicely washed and hemstitched, and a little trimming crocheted or knitted on the edge made them very attractive.

It was the custom to take an examination if you wanted to teach in the rural sections. I remember my first examination at the age of sixteen. Although too young to teach, I made my examination. My uncle, in Goochland County, stood for me and I was given a school, with much success. At the age of eighteen years, I applied in Henrico County after taking the examination under Mr. J. K. Fussell. I was appointed to old Mountain Road School.[1]

It is not difficult to picture this little wayside school, for although it has now disappeared, there are many such dotted about the Southern States. It was old, bare within and without, and stood on a roughly cleared patch of ground by the side of a hilly road in which the visitor's buggy would sink at times to the wheel hubs. Conditions here, it is true, were no better and no worse than in many another coloured school of the time, or even today, but to this quiet, determined eighteen-year-old girl they were a call to action. Listen to her account of how she improved the ground around her school.

[1] Most of the biographical material in this chapter was supplied by Miss Randolph, and the incidents related in autobiographical form have been reproduced as nearly as possible as they were described by her.

The first day I enrolled 14 pupils. The school was old and the grounds were nothing but a red clay hill. Having been taught to make the best of what you have, I began trying to improve conditions. I met with many obstacles from the beginning, as it was something new, but "Nothing is achieved without great labor," so I journeyed on. My first work was to try and improve the grounds. Mrs. Gary who lived just opposite the school, had a gravel pit. I went to her to buy gravel, but she said, "pay for the hauling, you may have the gravel." I had no money, but I organized a "Willing Workers Club," gave entertainments, and secured the necessary funds. After getting the yard level, my next thought was a green lawn. One of the oldest patrons in the community, Mrs. Valentine, gave me the lawn grass seed. I had a nice soil put on the ground and then sowed the grass. Before this, the ground was unsightly. I remember on many occasions, the School Board would go in mud to the hub of their buggy, trying to get to the school.

I saw in the paper where Governor Swanson had issued a proclamation for "Arbor Day." I waited until the time appointed, cut out the clipping, sent notices to the churches, had twelve of my patrons to bring trees and on that day in the presence of a large crowd, celebrated the first Arbor Day program held in Henrico County. The trees were named for the twelve Disciples. Mrs. Kate Minor, then in the State Library Building, thought it such a splendid idea, she said she would file one of the programs. The twelve trees lived and remained standing until we had to add on another room, and Judas stood in the way and had to be cut down.

It was some years before the additional room could be provided, and the early days at Mountain Road

School were taken up with more pressing problems. Indeed they were so full that it is difficult to do them justice, and to disentangle the many activities of this indefatigable young woman in what must have been an almost unending round of devoted toil. Soon, for example, her love of children and her womanly sympathies led her to visit the homes of her pupils, to find there conditions which saddened her, and aroused in her a desire to help. The sick she made her special care, and in one crowded home she found a young woman, Laurel by name, suffering from consumption, lying on a bed with dark and dirty coverings. What could Virginia do? She could not give sheets, and was much too tactful to suggest the need for cleanliness. But a few days later the children in her little school were delighted to learn that they were to be shown how to make dolls' beds and bed-clothes. Flour bags were brought to school, cut open and hemmed to make sheets. To the children who kept their work clean a piece of cotton flannel was given to make blankets (pink, blue, white), which the girls were taught how to adorn with feather-stitching. Then followed the making of straw mattresses, the collecting of suitable boxes for bedsteads, the making of rag dolls for the children who had no other kind, and, finally, the beds all clean, neat, and complete, were shown on Patrons' Day to parents whom eager children insisted on bringing to the school.

By this time local interest in "better bedding" was thoroughly aroused, and when visiting the homes of school patrons Miss Randolph suggested that they might combine "to lead a surprise on Laurel and carry her some fruit and sheets." The idea was welcomed, and the older women began to meet in the schoolroom at night to prepare the gift. Sheets were made from sugar bags and presented to the sick woman, and the first step in Virginia's campaign for "better homes" had been successfully taken. Her mother's teaching had not been in vain, for, as Virginia remarks, "A simple home life in early days makes you understand what can be done."

Nor had the lessons she learnt in Sunday School and Church been forgotten. At that time, as always, she was deeply religious, and felt that her children needed something more definite than could be taught in a public day school. So she organized a Sunday School in which, to quote her own words,

We had no Bibles or Hymn Books. We applied to the Chairman of the School Board, Mr. J. S. Bryan, for permission to have Sunday School, and his father, Mr. Joseph Bryan, hearing of it, sent us money for Bibles, books and an organ. I kept the Sunday School going the year round for five years, and walked nearly every Sunday from Lakeside to school and back, a distance of eight miles, during all kinds of weather.

Under Miss Randolph's patient care and guidance, therefore, a change gradually came over this little one-room school. A Patrons Improvement League was organized, the building was whitewashed and regularly swept and cleaned; vines and flowers soon gave it a bright appearance, a firm pathway made access easy

Mountain Road School, 1911: Old Building renovated and enlarged

Mountain Road School: New Building, dedicated 1915

from the high-road, and green lawns, trees, and shrubs still further enhanced the contrast between the old and the new. But it was uphill work, and although for the most part the County School Board was sympathetic, her own people and even her own school patrons were not always so. Sometimes she had to contend with angry parents whose mistaken zeal for their offspring led them to resent her innovations and particularly her discipline. Such, for example, was the woman who boasted that she "had whipped every teacher that had been at the school," and, as it turned out, was determined to repeat the performance. Her opportunity came when she learnt that her children had been punished for being concerned in a quarrel after school was over. Next day, towards the close of school, the angry mother appeared. What followed Virginia herself shall tell.

The children told me a lady was coming to the school, and by and by I saw a big woman standing in the porch with a long stick, taller than she. I was jus' praying, and was scared too. She said "I want to speak to you," and I answered, "Walk right in. I'll speak to you in a few minutes. Wait till we have devotions." We got ready for prayers, and it happened that the verses that day were from the 13th Chapter of Corinthians, and they were recited by the children. Then I said, "Children, this morning I'm going to pray, 'Lord have mercy on dear mother that come to school: so glad to see you, dear mother.'" I was scared to death and without waiting I said, "Let us sing, 'I need thee every hour.'" When the children had finished I said to them, "Now, children, I know you all feel proud that this is the first mother that has been to school. She is a mother with two lovely children and you know 'the hand that rocks the cradle rules the world.' Children, don't you feel proud? I'm going to ask her to speak to us." The mother was touched, and with tears in her eyes she said, "I came for one thing and I have found another: I'll never come to disturb the school any more." She kept her word, and became one of the school's Willing Workers. Soon afterwards she had a picture made of me, and hung it on the walls of her house.

At other times the young teacher met with more organized opposition. Thus, because there were no funds available for school improvement, money had to be raised by entertainments, and the necessary labour done by the children. This aroused a storm of protest among parents who thought that their children were sent to school to learn from books, and not to do manual labour. The opposition went so far that in the end a meeting was called at the local church and a petition signed asking that Virginia Randolph be removed. The church was crowded, Virginia was present but remained silent, and when the petition, very wisely, was ignored by the County Superintendent, her enemies vented their wrath on her in other ways. They tried, for example, to keep their children away from school, but, adds Virginia with a good-natured twinkle, "the children cried to come." The climax was reached on a certain Sunday evening in one of the local churches, when, after listening to insulting and insinuating remarks from the pulpit, Virginia was moved to rise and protest. She did so simply and with dignity. "We are here to help each other. I have been appointed by the School Board as a teacher and the church and school should be helping each other. If we are teaching right religion we should be helping each other. Insinuations don't help." That was all—the next morning she received an apology from the minister, and another of her many battles was over.

These incidents make it clear that the new teacher of Mountain Road School had ideas of her own about the appearance and discipline of a school, and had also the courage and initiative to put them into practice. This was equally true of the instruction to be given to the children. For Virginia Randolph the conception of education as the all-round development of the individual child was a simple truth which required no elaborate demonstration, and to a teacher with her aptitude and upbringing the introduction of work with the hands readily suggested itself. She made a start by devoting two afternoons a week "to doing anything that needed to be done"; she used her knowledge of sewing to teach the girls how to ply the needle, and with her usual thoroughness insisted that all needlework should be kept clean and done with care; she brought in honeysuckle and hickory from the woods to teach the boys how to make useful baskets. But she was not satisfied, and began to plan more ambitious schemes. Fearful, however, of what her own people might think of any further innovations, Miss Randolph thought it wise to see what white children were doing in their schools, and so it came about that one day "a small, slender, unassuming Negro woman knocked at the door of what she called a progressive school, and asked for help and suggestions to do for her people what a more fortunately situated group of white teachers were attempting to do for theirs."[2] "Pieces"—scraps of dress material and clothing—then discarded bits of reed and raffia, found their way from the more fortunate to the less fortunate school, for in those early days Virginia had to obtain her supplies as best she could, and often spent part of her meagre salary for this purpose. Only when she had satisfied herself that her new ventures were justified did she ask for help from public funds.

In these and other ways Miss Randolph, without neglecting the teaching of the usual school subjects, gradually enlarged the range and scope of what had by this time come to be known as "industrial education." She believed firmly in "learning by doing," and in honest work as the best of all character builders. The white teachers who helped her, and with whom she discussed her plans, were struck by her humility and eagerness to learn, but they soon found that she had an independent spirit. "She realised that, perhaps, she trespassed on the time of her white friends, and not infrequently asked if there was not something she could do. She was particularly proud of her laundry work and no greater pleasure could she have than 'to do up something for you' as she expressed it."[3]

[2] From a manuscript note by one of the teachers in this "progressive school."
[3] Manuscript note by one of the white teachers.

Gardening at Mountain Road School

Cooking class at Mountain Road School

VIRGINIA ESTELLE RANDOLPH

Thus by incessant toil, great determination, and an unselfishness and singleness of purpose which disarmed her critics, this slightly built Negro woman rallied the school patrons around her, and made her little school a centre of light and life in the community. The School Board for Henrico County became interested, and then helpful, and when in 1905, Jackson Davis, the newly appointed County Superintendent of Schools, visited Mountain Road School, he not merely recognized the worth of honest effort, but saw in the work of this teacher a practical expression of ideas already shaping in his own mind. "Here," as he said, "was a teacher who thought of her work in terms of the welfare of the whole community, and of the school as an agency to help the people to live better, to do their work with more skill and intelligence, and to do it in the spirit of neighborliness."[4] Surely, he thought, what has been accomplished here should be possible elsewhere.

But how was this to be brought about? The idea that first suggested itself to Jackson Davis was to arrange for Miss Randolph to visit other rural schools on one or two days a week, and to provide a substitute teacher for the Mountain Road School while she was so engaged. On such visits she could not only pass on to others in her own direct and simple fashion her ideas about education, but she could show the teachers themselves how to use their hands and organize their work. Unexpected difficulties arose—the other teachers were jealous; they criticized Miss Randolph's dress, hinted

[4] Pp. 15-16, *supra*.

that she had no special industrial training, objected to being shown like children how to do things, and particularly to Miss Randolph's taking any part in the instruction of their pupils. As one of them said, "The teacher should do all the teaching so that the children will not think the teacher does not know." The kindness, tact, and good humour of Miss Randolph usually won the day, but stronger measures were sometimes called for. "One big bright woman," she explains, "was very haughty," and in the end had to be spoken to by the County Board of Education.

Difficulties of this kind were not likely to deter one who had served so long and so arduous an apprenticeship in the hard school of experience, and who had faith in the changes she was advocating. A much greater difficulty arose when Miss Randolph was asked if she would devote the whole of her time to the work of supervision. She could not bring herself to leave the school in which she had laboured for so many years, and kept putting off her answer to Jackson Davis, from whom the suggestion had come. As she told me of her indecision, her dilemma seemed to come back to her vividly. "I prayed," she said, "for guidance. I'll go where you want me to go, dear Lord. I'll do what you want me to do." Next day the message went to Jackson Davis, "I have made up my mind to leave, and I'm going to leave to-day." She was as good as her word, and in October, 1908, she became the first Jeanes Teacher.

Miss Randolph's activities in this new sphere we

VIRGINIA ESTELLE RANDOLPH

shall describe in the next chapter. She has served continuously as the Supervisor of Negro Schools in Henrico County from 1908 to the present time, and her name and her work have become known not merely in her own country, but in other parts of the world. She has never lost touch with her old school, and has seen it grow from a one-room one-teacher school with fourteen pupils into the Virginia Randolph County Training School, with an enrolment of 235 pupils, of whom 75 are in the High School grades. To the original school building was added a kitchen, necessitating the removal of one of the twelve trees planted in early days and named after the twelve apostles—fortunately the offending tree turned out to be Judas Iscariot! As numbers increased other buildings became necessary and were erected beside the old schoolhouse, while in 1924 there was added the Jeanes Memorial Dormitory to provide residential accommodation for the older girls attending the school and better equipment for their instruction in Home Management. In 1929, the existing wooden buildings were destroyed by fire, and the entries in Miss Randolph's report for the month are illuminating:

February 11th: My school burned to the ground. The rest of the week I was unable to go anywhere. Under the care of the Doctor. I have worked so hard and just to think I could not save either building. God knows how I feel. I will never get over it.

February 18th: Getting the children adjusted ... We are a little overcrowded at the Virginia Randolph

School but owing to circumstances I think we are working out very well.[5]

So, indomitable as ever, she resumed her duties. The wooden buildings of the older school have been replaced by a large and commodious brick structure of modern design, but for me the pictures that will always remain most vivid will be of Virginia Randolph in the old school quietly superintending the preparation of a typical Southern meal in the school kitchen, or leading in prayer and praise some two hundred children of all ages tightly packed in its largest room.

What, we may ask, are the qualities which have enabled this "small, slender, unassuming Negro woman" to win through? Some of them have already been noticed, others are revealed by the incidents we have recorded—patience and faith, tact, kindliness, good humour, a humility that shows itself in her willingness to learn from others, and a quiet tenacity of purpose that overcomes all difficulties. But though humble she is independent, and though patient and tenacious she has not been lacking in enthusiasm and vigour. In 1926 the Harmon Foundation awarded her a prize for her contribution to education, and on the occasion of its presentation the Armstrong High School in Richmond was crowded to the doors with representative citizens of Richmond and Virginia. The Richmond Community Fund, through its president, John Stewart Bryan, gave her a silver loving-cup in appreciation of her serv-

[5] Manuscript report by Miss Virginia Randolph to the Jeanes Trustees, May, 1929.

Virginia Randolph County Training School:
Jeanes Memorial Dormitory

Physical exercises at the Virginia Randolph County
Training School

VIRGINIA ESTELLE RANDOLPH

ice to the Fund as a member of the Board of Management. The Virginia Randolph County Training School sent her a vase, and the Negro teachers of Henrico County gave her a silver pitcher. But withal she remains as simple-hearted and unassuming as ever.

Two striking tributes, from those who have known her best, may complete the picture. John Stewart Bryan, one of Miss Randolph's earliest supporters, writes:

Thirty years ago, as a member of the School Board for Brookland District, Henrico County, Virginia, I was visiting the various schools. On our rounds we stopped at a little school consisting of one room, and attended by Colored children. The teacher looked as if she had just stepped out of a bandbox, so spruce and spry was she, and her dress as spick and span and newly starched as if there was no such thing in the world as mud and rain. She came forward to receive us. This teacher was Virginia E. Randolph. I got that day the impression of the vigor and imagination, common sense and resourcefulness that has characterized this woman's extraordinary career.[6]

Finally, Jackson Davis in a few short sentences sums up the qualities which have made her not merely a successful Jeanes Teacher, but the type of all true teachers.

While many flattering things have been said about her by her friends, she maintains her simplicity and

[6] From a manuscript note by Mr. Bryan. Mr. Bryan as Editor of the Richmond *News-Leader* has been active in all progressive movements in Virginia for more than thirty years, and is now President of the College of William and Mary.

devotion. She is a leader by being a servant of all, and she has a genius for doing the simple little things that make up the larger things in education and in character. Her work in Henrico County is a shining light and example.[7]

[7] From the address given by Jackson Davis at the dedication of the Jeanes Memorial Dormitory, Henrico County Training School, Nov. 18th, 1924.

IV

EARLY DAYS

EXPERIMENT AND EXPANSION

WHEN THE Board of Trustees of the Jeanes Fund assembled for their first regular meeting in February, 1908, and appointed Dr. Dillard as their first president, neither he nor they had formulated any plans for carrying out the trust imposed upon them. The first few months, therefore, were devoted to a careful survey of the field and to making whatever special enquiries seemed advisable. Many requests for help were received, and also many letters offering suggestions—among them several from County Superintendents of Schools which were particularly welcome, for inasmuch as it was the expressed wish of Miss Jeanes that the income from the Fund should be used to help the small Negro rural school and practically all these were public schools, it was evident that the Trustees would have to work in close co-operation with local School Boards and their officers. It was not easy, however, to devise a scheme which would enable them to distribute the benefits of the limited amount of money at their disposal over so wide an area as the Southern States.

Their first experiment was suggested by a practice already adopted in certain cities, whereby a teacher trained in such subjects as sewing and woodwork went from school to school to give instruction in them. This seemed a suitable plan to adopt for country schools, and the introduction of "industrial subjects" was very much in accordance with the educational thought of the time. The first teacher to be employed in a rural area for this purpose and paid by the Jeanes Fund was Mrs. M. L. Sorrell, and her work lay in Iberville Parish, Louisiana, under the direction of the Parish Superintendent of Schools, L. E. Messick.[1] The plan adopted was that Mrs. Sorrell should have her headquarters at Plaquemine, the parish seat, work for two days a week in the Plaquemine Coloured School, and on the other three days visit five schools which were within fairly easy reach. This arrangement seemed to work quite well; other "extension teachers" were appointed in rural areas, and by the end of the session fifty of them were at work in various parts of the Southern States.[2] They threw themselves into their new duties with energy and enthusiasm, and by their success paved the way for subsequent developments.

In May, 1908, Dr. Dillard received from Jackson Davis the letter to which we have already referred, asking for the help of the Jeanes Fund in an experiment

---

[1] The parish in Louisiana corresponds to the county in other states.
[2] J. H. Dillard, *Fourteen Years of the Jeanes Fund*. Reprint from the *South Atlantic Quarterly*, XXII (July, 1923), 196-97.

Virginia Randolph County Training School:
New Building, 1930

Virginia Randolph at the entrance to the New Building
of the County Training School

EARLY EXPERIMENT AND EXPANSION 41

which he wished to make in Henrico County. This letter is so important that we must reproduce it in full.[3]

HENRICO PUBLIC SCHOOLS
Office of the Superintendent

Henrico Court House
Richmond, Va.

May 21, 1908

Dr. James H. Dillard,
 Chairman of the Board of the Jeanes Fund
 for Negro Education.

Dear Sir:

I am anxious to make industrial training an essential part of the work in the Negro schools of Henrico County. During the past session I have tried to interest our Negro teachers in this kind of work, and their response and co-operation has been so general as to lead me to believe that next session would be a most favorable time to begin the work in a systematic way. Many of the schools have organized Improvement Leagues in their communities and have made the school buildings and grounds more attractive in many ways. They have also made a beginning with various kinds of hand-work, such as sewing, making baskets of white-oak, mats of corn shucks, fishing-nets, brooms, &c., in every case using materials already at hand. They have gotten homes in some communities to agree to allow school children to come in at certain times each week for lessons in cooking.

The local school boards have become interested and will in one community consolidate their one-room

[3] From a copy supplied by Jackson Davis. The letter is also reprinted in Wright, *op. cit.*, p. 12.

Negro schools and erect a suitable building maintaining a graded school with equipment for industrial work. There will also be about ten acres of land attached for agriculture. In another community we have already consolidated two neighboring one-room schools and are co-operating with Dr. R. E. Jones and other prominent Negroes in maintaining a graded and industrial school. But these are only two centers and there will remain eighteen other Negro schools in the county—most of them one-room—with an enrollment of 700 pupils. We would like therefore to have in the county two teachers to supervise and direct the industrial work, going from school to school, meeting pupils and teachers. They would have their headquarters at the two industrial schools, but from these they would reach out to all the others. We estimate that we would have to pay these teachers about $40 a month, which would make $720 a year for the two.

While I have no doubt but that this movement will prove successful and would be a long step towards giving the Negro a true education, our local board feels that this year it can do no more than erect the building I spoke of, the demands of all the schools being unusually heavy just at this time. I therefore request your Board to assist us if possible in getting this work begun in our Negro schools. I believe that, if you would allow us the pay of two teachers for next session, the work would become self-sustaining after one year.

I may add that Dr. S. C. Mitchell and Dr. H. B. Frissell are acquainted with our work.

In the hope that this request will appeal to you favorably, I am

Respectfully yours,
Jackson Davis,
Supt. Schools.

EARLY EXPERIMENT AND EXPANSION

I cordially endorse the foregoing application of one of our most progressive and efficient division superintendents.

J. D. Eggleston, Jr.
Supt. Public Instruction

Richmond, Virginia
May 22, 1908.

The plans outlined by Jackson Davis in this letter were attractive in several ways. In the first place it would clearly be more economical for a teacher to visit a larger number of schools—for example, all the schools in a county—rather than confine her attention to a few. Then, in the second place, the idea of linking up school and community, which underlay the suggestions contained in the letter, seemed not only to be excellent in itself, but wholly in keeping with the spirit of Miss Jeanes's bequest, the more so as every effort was to be made to arouse the coloured people to help themselves. Finally, and in some ways most important of all, here was a County Superintendent of Schools whose initiative and foresight augured well for the experiment, and teachers who had already carried out in their own schools some of the improvements which it was hoped to bring about in many others. On June 4th, Dr. Dillard wrote to say that he would recommend to his Executive Committee that it pay the salary of one industrial teacher to work in the schools of Henrico County, Virginia, for the 1908-09 session. The recommendation was cordially approved by the Committee, and in October

Jackson Davis was able to write to Dr. Dillard to tell him of Miss Virginia Randolph's appointment as the industrial teacher for that county. The letter notifying Dr. Dillard of this appointment amplifies the suggestions contained in Mr. Davis's earlier communication, and runs as follows:[4]

> Henrico Court House
> Richmond, Va.
> October 26, 1908.
>
> Dear Dr. Dillard:
>
> I have secured Miss Virginia E. Randolph (colored), 813 Moore St., Richmond, as the industrial teacher for the Negro schools in the county, and her work in this field began today. I think we are fortunate in securing her, as she has had twelve years' experience in the public schools, and in her own school she has accomplished many of the results in industrial work that we now hope for in all the schools. She possesses common sense and tact in an unusual degree and has the confidence of all who know her, both among white people and those of her own race. We are a little late in starting, but I could not get her released from the school which she was teaching until this time. I called a meeting of the Negro teachers on the 23rd for the purpose of discussing the industrial work that we felt it would be practicable to undertake, and the outcome of the discussion was gratifying. I feel that they are all interested and will work faithfully to accomplish results. Our aim is to organize Improvement Leagues at each school and have the Negroes provide the equipment themselves. Several

---

[4] From a copy supplied by Mr. Jackson Davis. See also Wright, *op. cit.*, p. 18.

Home visits by Jeanes Teachers: Charles City County, Virginia, 1913

Virginia Randolph visits a rural school, about 1911

EARLY EXPERIMENT AND EXPANSION   45

schools have already begun this. I am sure that Virginia Randolph will direct this work in a way that will be most valuable on the principle of self-help, making use of whatever material may be at hand.

Her salary is forty dollars a month (four weeks), and I would like to ask how you wish to pay her, whether by direct check to her or through our School Board. I should also be glad if you would let me know what reports you would like to have as to her work and how often, etc.

Very truly yours,
Jackson Davis.

The result of this new experiment was awaited with interest by Dr. Dillard and his fellow Trustees, and at the end of the session W. Arthur Maddox, who had succeeded Jackson Davis as Superintendent of Schools for Henrico County, forwarded to them his observations and also a report prepared by Virginia Randolph herself.[5] "This simple report," says Dr. Dillard, "told the story so well in concrete terms that we printed a thousand copies and mailed them to county superintendents throughout the South."[6] It was a plain unvarnished record of services rendered and improvements effected in almost every school in Henrico County, but behind it lay the story of many a long and tiring day. Travelling in rural Virginia was by no means so comfortable and speedy as it is now rapidly becoming. To get to her

---

[5] Mr. Maddox served as Superintendent of Schools in Henrico County from February 1, 1909 to November 1, 1910, and rendered Miss Randolph invaluable assistance in organizing her work during this period.

[6] Dillard, *op. cit.*, p. 197. Miss Randolph's report is printed in full as Appendix A (pp. 127 to 132).

schools Miss Randolph was obliged to hire a one-horse buggy and driver, an expense which absorbed the greater part of her salary. Later, as she became more familiar with the district and more accustomed to driving, she bought a horse ("not a gala horse," she humorously adds) and went out alone. She had twenty-three schools to visit, and usually tried to reach two of them in a day. To do so she had to leave home at 6:30 A.M. and would arrive at the first school by 9:30. Then at 12:30 P.M. she would leave for the second school, and set off finally for home about 4 o'clock, hoping to arrive by 9 o'clock, and always finding her mother at the window anxiously awaiting her daughter's home-coming. The horse had to be fed and watered at suitable intervals (often the school children would help), the roads were so bad that at any moment her buggy might be stuck fast in the mud, and in winter she would sometimes be wet to the skin with rain and snow. But her enthusiasm and determination carried her through. The meeting of teachers to which Jackson Davis refers in his letter of October 26th to Dr. Dillard had been a great help in paving the way for her visits, and in working out the programme outlined in that letter she seized every opportunity that presented itself of arousing the interest and activity of parents, teachers, and children. "Anything hands find to do, I do," was her motto.

The circulation of Miss Randolph's report by the Trustees of the Jeanes Fund brought further letters from county superintendents of schools (particularly those in whose areas extension teachers of the earlier

EARLY EXPERIMENT AND EXPANSION 47

type were already working), asking that the new plan might be tried in their counties. It had been found that a teacher with headquarters at one school tended to give too much time to that school, and the arrangement adopted in Henrico County seemed to obviate this. The two systems were carefully compared, Dr. Dillard visited Henrico County to satisfy himself as to the value of the second experiment, and gradually, during the next two years, the existing extension teachers all became supervising industrial teachers either for a whole county or for part of a county. A few County Boards of Education began to assist by making small grants in aid of transportation, and by the following session (1909-10) 129 Jeanes Teachers were at work in 130 counties of 13 Southern States. The number dropped to 98 in the following year, as rather less money was available, but rose steadily in succeeding years; during the session 1913-14 Jeanes Teachers to the number of 118 were employed by 119 counties, 29 of them being men and 89 women.[7] The idea had evidently appealed to those responsible for rural coloured schools.

Who were these Supervising Industrial Teachers? Where had they been trained and what did they do for the schools under their charge? Most of them were teachers of experience who, like Virginia Randolph, had already made good in the public schools. About half of them had been educated at Hampton or Tuskegee Institute or at other normal and industrial schools. The

---

[7] Jeanes Fund, Report of President, 1914, gives statistical details for years 1908 to 1914. *See also* Appendix D, p. 143.

remainder had received no specific training in industrial work; to quote one of them, "I was trained at no industrial school. I got the first principles with other training." Their activities were as varied as the needs of the schools, industrial work, naturally, looming rather large in their earlier reports—plain sewing, darning, cooking, agriculture, gardening, blacksmithing, carpentry, chair seating, hammock making, shuck mat making all are mentioned—and such activities as singing, paper-cutting, and drawing are occasionally noted. Only in one or two reports is there any reference to the more usual school subjects.

But in spite of the novelty and importance of industrial work in the schools the chief interest of these early reports is to be found in the many other activities which they reveal. Thus a Jeanes Teacher in Alabama, typical of others, reported that she had found it necessary to concentrate on school building and repairs, while a Mississippi teacher noted with pride that the yard of one school had been levelled and beautified with shrubs, the windows washed, a shelf put up to hold the water pail, two wash pans bought, and towels made by the older girls. The pride of another teacher was in a "new pump and a new flew."[8] Or again, a Louisiana supervisor reported that in April he visited homes to take an "Education Census," and gave a talk to the School Board, while a supervisor in North Carolina lectured to 500 persons on the danger of tuberculosis, particularly to people engaged in industry. Sev-

[8] The spelling of the report.

EARLY EXPERIMENT AND EXPANSION 49

eral reported the lengthening of the school term, the organization of School Improvement Leagues, and a growing interest on the part of parents in the school work of their children. One supervisor gleefully reported that "Some of the patrons came to two of the schools during the recent industrial period and became so impressed that they went home and sent some more children just to have them learn the industries," while another added, "Each visit the parents spend a deal of time with the children and take part in the work. I usually address the parents and children together and am exceedingly pleased with the interest and progress of parents and children." A happy state of affairs which many a teacher will envy!

Finally we may note that, like Virginia Randolph, these early Jeanes Teachers were not indifferent to the home conditions under which their pupils lived. One man, more ambitious and with greater facilities than the rest, reported the making of washstands, tables, wheelbarrows, clothes-hangers and "numerous other articles of usefulness," another that "the homes of the people have been enlarged and beautified." More graphic in its directness, but more truly representative of the simple character of the services rendered, is the report that "One house had only two windows. It now has four nice large windows." Progress was slow and the approach to the home had to be made through the school.

There were many difficulties to be overcome. Here it was a recalcitrant school principal whose objections were over-ruled by "enthused" parents; elsewhere the "Committee and Patrons do not favour introducing industrial features in public schools." Or again, a supervisor complained that "on account of the incompetency of the County Teachers and difficulty found in travelling the work is not carried out in the different village schools," and from another supervisor come reports of communities where "little interest is shown," "nothing is done," and of one district in which someone has "burned down the school." But the prevailing note is one of optimism, and there is at times a refreshing naïveté about the reports, as well as an amusing quaintness in their phraseology. Thus we are told by one Jeanes Teacher that "The interest shown, the condition of schools, the great need of this phase of training, propels me on." Another rhetorically proclaims the need of his people. "All these places desire help from the Fund. The people in this State and County need immediate salvation. We are weak. Great is the harvest. Few are labouring." To a third the public speaking which the Jeanes work entails is a delight. "Lectured, it seems to their delight" runs one sentence in his report, and he adds that this has been "The most pleasant year's work of my life. I have had the pleasure of speaking to my people as never before upon a subject that will do much to inspire and lift them up intellectually, industrially, and morally." Truly both his heart and his tongue were unloosed. Finally, more simply, but with evident sincerity, we are told by a woman supervisor who has organized a Willing Workers League that "they

An unimproved rural home

An improved rural home
Additional windows have been inserted; a porch (or verandah) added, and a one-story annex built at the rear.

EARLY EXPERIMENT AND EXPANSION 51

always meet me with pleasure and I am also glad to be among them."

The methods which these pioneers employed were as varied as the services which they rendered. Sometimes a patrons' meeting would be arranged to take place at the school, and frequently in preparation for this the Jeanes Teacher would devote part of her time to a round of home visits. Sunday services at the local churches would be attended, occasionally, no doubt, for the convenience of speaking to the congregation on matters relating to the school—but more usually because many Jeanes Teachers were deeply religious and were glad to join the community in worship and prayer, or to help by teaching in the Sunday School. They organized Improvement Leagues and Mothers Clubs, arranged concerts and entertainments in order to raise funds, and frequently helped teachers to plan school commencement exercises so as to serve the double purpose of ending the session effectively, and of rallying public interest and support to the school. Often the first task of the Jeanes Teacher was to seek out the local trustees of the school and arouse them to a sense of their responsibilities. If they were already interested in the school, she would co-operate with them in finding ways and means of improving the building, or providing a schoolhouse where none existed and the school was held in a lodge hall or in a church.

Within and around the school the Jeanes Teachers taught rather by example than precept. They were the leaders in "cleaning up," and took part in the actual instruction, particularly in industrial subjects. They were greatly handicapped by lack of materials and by a poverty which made it difficult for either the pupils or their parents to bear the cost of providing them. What little money was available or could be raised often had to be used to provide the bare necessities of school life—blackboards, or even seats for the children. The fact is that many a Negro public school in the rural South comprised little more than a building and a teacher, and the Jeanes Teachers had to begin by giving help when and where it was most urgently needed.

To get to the schools they had to overcome difficulties of transport, the roads in many parts of the South being worse even than those in Virginia. But their courage and ingenuity were equal to the task. Where distances permitted, and no means of conveyance was available, they walked from school to school, carrying with them food, and often, too, materials for industrial work. At other times patrons of one school would arrange for a buggy to convey the teacher to another, or to her home. Even those Supervisors who were fortunate enough to possess a horse and buggy could not be sure that they would be able to arrive at their destination, particularly after heavy rains, and it must have needed a stout heart to venture forth day after day in all weathers under such circumstances as these.[9]

[9] This account of their early activities is based on the monthly reports of Jeanes Supervisors to the Jeanes Trustees.

EARLY EXPERIMENT AND EXPANSION

From the first Dr. Dillard kept in close touch with both County Superintendents and Jeanes Teachers, and his intimate knowledge of conditions and of people in the South enabled him to interpret their monthly reports with sympathy and understanding. For a time he refrained from issuing any formal instructions to the Jeanes Teachers, but in 1911, when he felt that the time had come to give them a little guidance, he sent to each of them a letter, in which, carefully avoiding detailed instructions, he put before them the principles which should guide them in their work, and praised the spirit in which that work had been undertaken. The letter is as follows:

I take this means of addressing each one of you on the subject of our work. You are one of a body of workers whose salaries are paid by this Fund for the purpose of enabling you to devote whatever ability and skill you possess, and all your most earnest efforts, to the betterment of the rural schools and communities of your race in our Southern States. You know, in a general way, that our desire is for you to do whatever you can for school and neighbourhood improvement in the communities which may be reached by you. Purposely you have not been given very specific rules and directions, and this for two reasons. First, the work of this Fund is new both in time and in plan. It is necessary to learn gradually the best way of doing things, so that the work may be intelligent as well as earnest. Second, conditions vary from State to State, from county to county and even from community to community. The kind and method of work best suited to one place may not be suitable in another place. For this reason it is to be expected that the reports which you make each month should show considerable difference in the character of work.

You can see that it would be difficult to prescribe precisely what each worker should do, but enough is known to guide you in the main lines. You should keep in touch with the school officials and show that you desire to work in accord with them. You should exercise tact and discretion in dealing with the teachers of the schools which you visit, and show that you have no desire to usurp authority, but wish to be a helper and fellow-worker. You should assist in organizing the people of the community into associations for self-help, for school improvement, for extension of terms, for sanitation or any other good purpose. You should co-operate with the minister or ministers of the community, and thus endeavour to bring the great influence of the churches to bear upon the practical life of the people. You should introduce into the schools such simple forms of industrial work as may be needful and helpful, and will tend to show the connection between the school and the daily life of the community. You should by word and example endeavour to promote orderliness, promptness, and cleanliness, being particularly careful, for the sake of the influence on the children, that the school-rooms and school surroundings, no matter how poor, be kept neat and tidy, and in as good condition as possible. You should urge and demand care and accuracy in the work which you supervise, remembering that one good purpose of such training is to prevent the doing of things in a slovenly way.

While, as has been said, your reports show that you are not all working in the same way, yet it seems true that all of you are doing good in the various places in which your work lies. On the whole it appears that those of you who are doing no actual teaching yourselves, except through the local teachers, are accomplishing more than those who are teaching the children yourselves; but I write now not in the spirit of criticism. I wish rather to express gratification at the zeal and earnestness and missionary spirit which so many are showing. You seem zealous in embracing the opportunity of doing something for the welfare, improvement, and encouragement of those who stand in need of better training and better advantages. If you have not this spirit, you should not be in this work.[10]

This wise and helpful letter would, I am sure, have rejoiced the heart of Miss Anna Jeanes. It represented the considered judgment of Dr. Dillard on what he had seen and heard of the results of three years' experiment, and determined the main lines of activity of the Jeanes Teachers for many years. The first group must have been a remarkable set of men and women, and most of them had already shown powers of leadership in their local communities. Some of them, like Virginia Randolph, are still faithfully carrying out their duties, and in talking with them it is possible to recapture something of the atmosphere of those early days, and sense the qualities which led them to undertake the work. They were carefully selected, and well deserved the tribute paid them by Dr. Dillard in 1923:

[10] The letter has been reprinted by the John F. Slater Fund in *Occasional Papers, No. 27 (Selected Writings of James Hardy Dillard).*

There are no words too strong to express the admiration which anyone who has known the Jeanes Teachers must feel for the ability and devotion they have shown in their work. There have been no nobler pioneers and missionaries than these humble teachers. They have literally gone about doing good.[11]

[11] Dillard, *op. cit.*, p. 198.

V

Progress by Co-operation

WITH THE general acceptance of the county as a basis for organizing the supervision of Negro rural schools, and the issue by Dr. Dillard of a letter of guidance and encouragement to Jeanes Teachers, the educational movement we are describing may be regarded as well under way. It would be interesting and pleasant to dwell at length on the adventures and achievements of the earnest pioneers to whom Dr. Dillard's words were addressed, but enough has been said to reveal their enterprise, resourcefulness and courage, and we must pass to a consideration of the work being done by their successors, the Jeanes Teachers of today. Before doing so, however, it will be advisable to examine from a somewhat different standpoint the educational movement of which they were the spearhead. Both in their inception and in their subsequent development the activities sponsored by the Jeanes Fund have been the result of co-operation, and have in turn led to other co-operative enterprises. It is this aspect of the movement which we propose to examine briefly in the present chapter.

The first experiment in Henrico County, Virginia, was made possible, as we have seen, by the co-operation of three groups of people. The County Superintendent suggested a scheme for the supervision of Negro schools, and with the approval and support of his School Board put it into operation; the President of the Jeanes Fund and his fellow Trustees welcomed the experiment and provided the salary of the first Jeanes Teacher; while patrons of rural schools in Henrico County, by their efforts to raise money and in other ways bring about school improvement, introduced an element of self-help without which the scheme would have been no more than a novel form of charitable assistance. To these three co-operating parties there was added, in the following year a fourth—a State Supervisor of Coloured Schools—and, very appropriately, this new and responsible post was first held by Jackson Davis.

The idea of a state supervisor for the coloured schools of Virginia originated with Dr. Frissell of Hampton, who realised how greatly Negro schools would be helped if in the State Department of Education there were some one person charged with their oversight and eager to promote their improvement. He therefore enlisted the interest and support of Dr. Wycliffe Rose, at that time General Agent of the Peabody Fund, and early in 1910 suggested to State Superintendent Eggleston that Mr. Jackson Davis should be assigned the special task of supervising Negro schools throughout the state; Dr. Frissell also advised Mr. Jackson Davis to accept such an appointment if it were offered. The upshot of these

PROGRESS BY CO-OPERATION 59

conversations was that in May, 1910, Jackson Davis became State Supervisor of Coloured Schools in Virginia, the necessary salary being provided by the Peabody Fund and the Southern Education Board. A year later Dr. Frissell interested Dr. Wallace Buttrick of the General Education Board in the scheme, and as the activities of the Peabody Fund were soon to cease,[1] it was arranged that the General Education Board should take over the financing of this new educational officer. Indeed the Board went further and offered to support Supervisors for Negro schools in other states, an offer quickly taken advantage of by Kentucky, Arkansas, Alabama, North Carolina, and Georgia, and today State Agents for Negro Schools (as they are usually called) are to be found in fifteen Southern States, in some cases at the head of a separate Division of Negro Education.[2] Their position has made them key men, for in all matters relating to the education of the Negro they are the principal representatives of their states, and the work of the Jeanes Teachers comes under their immediate supervision. They are Southern white men, usually of wide experience, and often of outstanding personality. Their salaries, together with an allowance for expenses, are provided by the General Education Board, but they are in all cases state officers appointed by the State Superintendent of Education. They have played a vital part in the development not merely of rural school supervision, but of all forms of public education for

[1] The Peabody Fund was dissolved in 1914.
[2] In 1933 the number of State Agents was 24—two Agents in each of nine states, and one in each of the remainder.

coloured people, and a leading Southerner recently paid them a well-merited tribute:

As part of the effort to develop an indigenous educational system for Negroes in the South probably no single factor has been more important than the work of the state agents.... There is much in the South to humiliate one but I never think of these state agents and their work without a feeling of pride. The South has produced nothing finer and more important than these men. They are today the pioneer leaders in the advance of Negro education.[3]

The appointment of State Agents marks a definite stage in the development of closer co-operation between the various groups of people interested in Negro education. Their strategic position and educational experience made them singularly well fitted to advise and help the trustees of any fund or agency interested in Negro schools, and because of their local knowledge they could ensure that public and private resources were wisely used. The Jeanes Fund also, being primarily concerned with rural schools—which then, as now, provide for the majority of coloured people—became a channel through which gifts from other philanthropic agencies were made to these schools, and the connections thus established were still further strengthened by the fact that at various times trustees of the Jeanes Fund were also trustees or members of executive committees of other funds. Indeed the inter-related activities so

[3] W. W. Alexander, *The Slater and Jeanes Funds: An Educator's Approach to a Difficult Social Problem* (John F. Slater Fund, Occasional Papers, No. 28), p. 15.

Dr. Dillard, Mr. W. T. B. Williams, and Mr. Jackson Davis, 1921

Mr. Jackson Davis and Dr. Dillard

PROGRESS BY CO-OPERATION 61

briefly summarized provide an example of concentrated co-operation which it would be difficult to parallel, and although it is unnecessary for our present purpose to describe the resulting co-operative activity in great detail, a few illustrative examples will help the reader to appreciate its significance.

The most striking example of the way in which the Jeanes Fund has become a channel through which financial aid has found its way to rural schools is the continued support received by the Jeanes Trustees from the General Education Board. Shortly before making her final gift of one million dollars to the small rural schools, Miss Anna Jeanes entrusted a sum of $200,000 to the General Education Board to be used for Negro rural schools in the South, and the income from this sum has been used in consultation with Hampton Institute and Tuskegee Institute to assist in providing better salaries for selected teachers, and for school buildings and equipment. At the same time generous additional grants from the Board to the Jeanes Trustees have enabled them not merely to increase the number of supervising teachers, but also to organize conferences of Jeanes Teachers, and to help individual supervisors attend summer schools—all this in addition to financial help and expert guidance given by the Board year after year to private schools and colleges throughout the South.[4] The effectiveness of the co-operation between the two organizations was still further ensured when

[4] The contribution of the General Education Board to the Jeanes Fund for the year ending June 30, 1932, amounted to $75,943.88. Wright, *op. cit.*, p. 169; see also Appendix D, Table V.

in 1915 Mr. Jackson Davis was appointed by the General Education Board to be their Field Agent specially concerned with Negro schools, an appointment which he held until he became one of the Board's principal officers.[5]

An experiment in co-operation of rather a different kind was initiated when in December, 1910, Dr. J. H. Dillard, President of the Jeanes Fund, became also General Agent of the Slater Fund.[6] Both funds, as we have seen, were concerned solely with the furtherance of Negro education, and for twenty-five years before the Jeanes Fund came into existence the Slater Fund had been assisting private and denominational schools as well as selected public schools for Negroes in the South. When, however, the Jeanes Supervisors had been at work for a year or two, it became evident that better teachers were sorely needed for the small rural schools, and in 1911 Dr. Dillard, in his capacity as chief executive officer of the Slater Fund, was asked if the Fund could help in developing central schools in certain counties of Virginia, Louisiana, Arkansas, and Mississippi. He saw at once that such schools might be the means of providing better educated teachers for primary schools. The immediate result was that in the school

[5] Jackson Davis became first an Assistant Director and later an Associate Director of the General Education Board. He was succeeded as Field Agent for the Board by Leo M. Favrot of Louisiana.

[6] In the work of the Slater Fund Dr. Dillard was ably assisted by W. T. B. Williams as Field Agent. Mr. Williams is a graduate of Harvard University, and in 1934 received the Spingarn Medal because of his outstanding achievement in Negro leadership. He is now vice-president of the College Department at Tuskegee Institute, and has been well described as a "Southern educator of the highest rank."

PROGRESS BY CO-OPERATION 63

year 1911-12 the Slater Fund gave the sum of $500 towards the salary of an industrial teacher for a Parish Training School for coloured children at Kentwood in Tangipahoa Parish, in the piney woods area of Louisiana.[7] Land and timber for the school were given by a lumber company, and the responsibility for furnishing teachers and equipment was shouldered by the local School Board. Three other schools were similarly helped by the Slater Fund in the same year,[8] and in subsequent years the plan was extended.

The idea was, to quote Dr. Dillard's words, to have in a county "at least one well-graded school, to which the best pupils might go from the little one-room schools and in which there might be some instruction and training for the preparation of teachers for the small schools of the county."[9] These new schools came to be known as County Training Schools, a name suggested by State Superintendent Eggleston of Virginia,[10] and from 1921 onwards they became the major interest of the Slater Fund. Between the years 1911 and 1932 no less than 612 schools have been aided as County Training Schools by the Slater Trustees, and many of them have become fully accredited four-year public high schools. In the year 1932-33 the number of schools aided by the Slater

---

[7] Edward E. Redcay, *County Training Schools and Public Secondary Education for Negroes in the South* (John F. Slater Fund, *Occasional Papers*, No. 29), p. 28.
[8] At Newton County, Mississippi; Hempstead County, Arkansas; and in Sabine Parish, Louisiana. *Ibid.*, pp. 29-30.
[9] *Selected Writings of James Hardy Dillard*, p. 13.
[10] *Ibid.*, p. 16.

Trustees was 356, enrolling more than 170,000 pupils, of whom 16,389 were in secondary grades.[11]

This remarkable development has undoubtedly led to an improvement in the academic attainments of the younger and more recently appointed teachers in small rural schools, and to this extent the work of the Jeanes Supervisor has been made easier. At first an attempt was made to include in the curriculum for the higher grades in County Training Schools some special preparation for teaching, as well as industrial activities, but as the years went by attention was concentrated more and more on improving the standard of academic work, high school grades being added with a view to eventual recognition as accredited rural high schools; Louisiana, indeed, appears to be the only state which still uses some of these schools for the purpose of training teachers.[12] Sometimes these larger and more adequately equipped schools have been useful centres from which the Jeanes Supervisor has been able to plan her round of school visits, and at which she has from time to time assembled the teachers in her district for conference. But no uniform plan of co-operation has been devised, and as the emphasis in County Training Schools has been placed increasingly on the development of work at the secondary level, the connection has become less close. The common administration of the Jeanes and Slater Funds, however, has encouraged an informal linking up of their activities wherever possible, and

---

[11] Redcay, *op. cit.*, p. 107.
[12] *Ibid.*, p. 97.

A one-room rural school

A four-teacher consolidated school: Rosenwald Building

PROGRESS BY CO-OPERATION

fortunately, since Dr. Dillard's retirement in 1931, this joint administration has continued under the capable guidance of Arthur D. Wright, also a Virginian, a graduate of the College of William and Mary, and of Harvard University, and from 1915 to 1920 State Agent for Negro Schools in Virginia.[13]

A third example of co-operative enterprise is seen in the steps by which many districts in the South have been provided with better school buildings. Letters to Dr. Dillard from Jeanes Teachers in every state emphasized the poor condition of the buildings in which rural schools were held, and in his reports to the Trustees for 1913 and 1914 we find him dwelling on the great need for improvement. "There is a tremendous need of betterment," he wrote. "It is hard to imagine the rudeness and dilapidation of the buildings in which nearly all of the country schools are held. In such places how can neatness and orderliness and thrift be satisfactorily taught?" Later, turning to the practical aspects of the problem, he adds,

We are beginning to have urgent appeals from the supervising teachers for help in school-house improvement in their various counties. These appeals come with the approval of the County Superintendents and frequently with offer of some contribution from the public funds.... I would strongly recommend that our Board should set aside five or even ten thousand dollars annually for this purpose but for the fact of the great need and demand for the supervising teachers.[14]

[13] From 1921 to 1931 Mr. Wright was Professor of Education at Dartmouth College.
[14] Jeanes Fund, Report of President, 1914, pp. 4-5.

Welcome aid towards the improvement of school buildings was offered by the Phelps-Stokes Fund, which had already in 1911-12 made a generous grant of $2,500 in aid of salaries from its none too large resources. To this gift was added in 1912-13 a sum of $1,000, and in 1913-14 a sum of $1,500, to help in providing school buildings.[15] But far larger resources were needed, and came in the form of timely aid from Julius Rosenwald of Chicago. In June, 1910, after a period of collaboration in school building with Booker T. Washington of Tuskegee, Mr. Rosenwald announced his intention of continuing the experiment, and offered to assist in the erection of 100 school buildings for Negroes in rural areas. Similar offers were made by him in February and November, 1912, and finally on October 30, 1917, the Julius Rosenwald Fund was incorporated under the laws of the State of Illinois. Between 1913 and 1933, when the school building programme of the Fund came to an end, no less than 5,357 individual schoolhouses had been built in fifteen Southern States, a valuable contribution to the cause of Negro education.[16] Equally important was the high standard set by the Rosenwald Trustees in planning buildings erected under their auspices. Plans and specifications were prepared by skilled architects, embodying the most modern ideas on school construction and providing also for community needs. These were available not only for the building of Rosenwald schools but, through State De-

[15] Dillard, *op. cit.*, p. 199.
[16] Edwin R. Embree, ed., *Julius Rosenwald Fund: Review for the Two-Year Period, 1931-1933*, p. 29.

PROGRESS BY CO-OPERATION 67

partments of Education, for the use of any community wishing to erect a new and modern school building. By their example and influence the Trustees have set up under the direction of their Southern agent, S. L. Smith, a new standard for school buildings throughout the South.

In this programme of school improvement State Agents for Negro Schools played an active part, and their efforts were in many cases energetically seconded by County Superintendents of Schools. Most of the work in the immediate locality, however, fell on the shoulders of the Jeanes Supervisors. It was they who called attention to the urgency of the need, and it was they who aroused the local community to play its part, and kept interest and enthusiasm alive until each school building project had been carried to a successful issue. Indeed it is impossible to read a batch of their reports to Dr. Dillard without noticing how patiently and persistently they strove for better school buildings in their districts; from their own experience as teachers they knew how greatly improvement in physical conditions would help in the other aspects of school life.

Underlying the co-operative activities we have thus briefly illustrated were two important principles enunciated very clearly by Dr. Dillard at one of the early meetings of the Jeanes Trustees. After emphasizing the need for a careful preliminary study of the rural school situation in the South he continued:

While bearing in mind this general caution we may venture to present two features of our future policy which have thus far commended themselves to us.

First, we believe that any definite work and assistance undertaken by us should be carried on with the approval and co-operation of the regular public school officials. There are already abundant indications of opportunity for developing our work under the sanction of the school authorities, and we believe that in this way we shall best promote the cause of equitable appropriations as well as the activity of local efforts.

Secondly, we believe that there are indications over the whole country of a movement for the re-organization of rural schools, to the intent that they may become more fully adapted to the needs of rural life. This problem is one which especially affects the South, where the population is so largely rural, and it directly faces us at the beginning of the administration of this Fund. It seems that we have a peculiar opportunity for working out this problem of effective training for rural life, and that immediate efforts may well be made in this direction.[17]

With the second of these principles and its attempted application by the Jeanes Teachers in their work we shall be concerned later. The first principle is well illustrated by the fact that the total amount expended on school building from public sources and from contributions made by the Negroes themselves has exceeded the amount contributed by the Rosenwald Fund, and the buildings so erected have become in each case the property of the authority responsible for the public school system.[18] In the Jeanes work also this same principle

---

[17] Wright, *op. cit.*, p. 37.

[18] For the whole period the contributions from various sources were as follows: Julius Rosenwald Fund $4,364,869; Negroes, $4,725,871; whites, $1,211,975; public funds, $18,105,805. Embree, *op. cit.*, p. 32.

PROGRESS BY CO-OPERATION 69

of co-operation with public authorities found expression from 1911 onwards, when County School Committees began to assist in the transport of Jeanes Teachers, as well as to provide funds for various forms of school improvement other than the erection or repair of buildings. By 1917-18 Dr. Dillard was able to report to his Trustees that counties were contributing towards the salaries and expenses of Jeanes Teachers an amount equivalent to approximately three-quarters of the sum contributed by the Jeanes Fund,[19] while in 1932 it was estimated that the expenditure from public funds and other sources for Jeanes work was no less than 66 per cent of the total expenditure, i.e., almost twice as much as the amount contributed by the Jeanes Trustees.[20] There has at no time been a fixed basis for contributions from these various sources, and the proportion of salary borne respectively by the Jeanes Fund, the county, and the state, has varied and still varies within very wide limits. As a general rule the contribution of the Jeanes Fund is greater in the poorer and more populous areas, in some cases representing the major part of the salary; elsewhere the position may be reversed. The elasticity which has always characterized the administration of the Fund has been a great help in dealing with areas widely differing in needs and financial resources, and the increasing willingness of some states and counties to share the burden has made expansion possible elsewhere. One state, Maryland, has

---

[19] Wright, *op. cit.*, p. 89.
[20] *Ibid. See also* Appendix D, Tables IV and VI.

taken over entirely the provision of Supervisors for Negro Rural Schools; several parishes in Louisiana, aided by the state, support the Jeanes work entirely from public funds; and there are signs that further progress may be expected along these lines.

The activities promoted by the Jeanes Fund have from the first reflected the wide interests of its Trustees. Here the extension of a school term has been made possible, elsewhere a few carefully selected books have been supplied to the isolated rural teacher. Conferences of various kinds have been promoted, preachers' institutes organized, an illiteracy campaign aided by a small but timely grant, and a Jeanes Memorial Dormitory erected in 1924 at the Henrico County Training School—Virginia Randolph's old school. Again, the close connection of the Trustees with other aspects of Southern life has ensured that, as Dr. Dillard once suggested, their interests would have a wider range than simply the management of the Fund. Thus it came about that at their meeting on June 23, 1911, the Trustees discussed and approved a suggestion for the formation of a University Commission on Race Relations, and appointed a committee of three to take up the question.[21] Their efforts led to the first meeting at Nashville, on May 9, 1912, of the University Commission on Race Relations in the South, the meeting being held in connection with the Southern Sociological Congress.[22] Eleven delegates from as many Southern

[21] Wright, *op. cit.*, p. 58.
[22] *Ibid.*, p. 65. A further Organization Meeting was held on May 24, 1912.

Mr. B. C. Caldwell with a class of rural ministers

Dr. Dillard confers with a Negro deacon at a preachers' institute

state universities were present, further meetings and conferences were held in subsequent years, and without doubt the work of this Commission has been one of the most educative influences in the history of the South.

With this final example of co-operation our chapter must close. The success of the enterprises we have described has been due in part to the ability and statesmanship of those responsible for their inception, but in large measure also to the courage and devotion of those who in humbler spheres have laboured to bring them to fruition. Their example has been an inspiration to many, and the quiet challenge of their efforts to meet the needs of the coloured people has done more than anything else to arouse the South to a sense of its responsibility. The Jeanes Teachers, in daily contact with the schools and moving constantly in and out of the homes of their people, have played a part in many, indeed in most, of the reconstruction movements of recent years, and to them and their activities we must now return.

VI

THE JEANES TEACHER AT WORK

As soon as the effectiveness of rural school supervision had been demonstrated by the pioneer Jeanes Teachers the idea spread very quickly through the South, and expansion was limited only by the amount of money available. In 1913 the number of Supervisors was 122; by 1919-20 it had risen to 218; and in 1930-31 no less than 329 Jeanes Teachers were in the field. Since then the United States, and the Southern States in particular, have been passing through a period of acute economic depression, but in spite of this, and the necessity for drastic retrenchments of every kind, it has been found possible to keep the number of Jeanes Supervisors fairly constant.[1] No doubt this has been due in some measure to the fact that part of their salary is paid by the Jeanes Fund, but it may also with reason be regarded as a tribute to their usefulness. Their work, it is true, has been made increasingly difficult by the economic depression, but they have bravely carried on, and it is the purpose of this and the succeeding chapter to

---

[1] With the passing of the economic depression the number of Jeanes Teachers has risen steadily, and for the year 1936-37 the total number employed is 426.

explain more fully the nature of their activities, after noticing briefly one or two facts relating more particularly to the conditions under which they work.

First of all we may note that, with few exceptions, the Jeanes Teachers today are women, often married women or widows.[2] Some of those who began work in the early days are still serving and are now between fifty and sixty years of age; the majority are between the ages of thirty-five and fifty, while several of those recently appointed are between the ages of twenty-five and thirty. In almost all cases the Supervisor has had previous experience as a teacher,[3] and about half of them have been educated, either wholly or in part, at State Normal Schools or at private schools like Hampton or Tuskegee. Until recent years this would usually have meant that they had been trained in industrial subjects, but of late there has been an increasing freedom of choice in the curriculum of these schools, with the result that the extent to which their graduates have received such training varies considerably. The remaining Supervisors (that is, about half the total number) have attended only high schools or colleges with purely academic curricula. An increasing number, however, have completed a course of preparation for teaching in elementary schools, while a few have subsequently added special courses in rural school supervision. Indeed, most Supervisors are desirous of improving their

[2] Of 303 Jeanes Teachers at work early in 1933-34 only 17 were men; of the women 177 were married or widows, and 109 were unmarried.
[3] Wright, *op. cit.*, p. 19, estimates an average of six years' experience as teachers, but there are wide variations.

academic or professional qualifications and attend summer schools, which as a rule devote particular attention to the problems of teaching in elementary grades.[4] It may safely be claimed, therefore, that the majority of Jeanes Teachers are by education, as well as by training and experience, superior to those whom it is their duty to supervise, although it would be too much to assert that they are all highly qualified.

Secondly, it is important to realise the wide variations in the conditions under which they work. For example, the percentage and also the actual number of Negroes varies greatly from county to county, and so therefore does the number of schools for Negro children, as well as the size and type of school—one-teacher, two-teacher, three-teacher. If we take as our basis of comparison the number of teachers with whom each Supervisor has to co-operate, we find, for example, that in Virginia this ranges all the way from 15 to 116, and in Alabama from 22 to 252, the larger numbers being more usual in the thickly populated counties of the Black Belt,[5] or in the delta sections of Mississippi.[6]

Another difference is to be seen in the number of months in each year for which the Jeanes Supervisor is engaged. In a state where there is some central control

[4] Summer schools in 1929 were attended by 21,659 Negro teachers.

[5] An area stretching from East to West across the centre of the South Atlantic States, comprising the greater part of South Carolina and the central portions of Georgia and Alabama. The name is usually associated in people's minds with the colour of the inhabitants, but was probably due in the first instance to the colour of the soil in the more fertile sections.

[6] The term delta is commonly used to denote the whole of the alluvial Mississippi Valley and not merely the mouth of the river.

Two-teacher rural school in poor area: principal and a group of over-age pupils

A progressive teacher and her pupils

THE JEANES TEACHER AT WORK 75

over the school system, there may be little or no variation from county to county. Thus, in Virginia for the year 1933-34, the engagement of Supervisors was for eight months, except in some half dozen counties where the locality agreed to extend the engagement for another month at its own expense. Similarly, in Louisiana only four engagements were for less than ten months, whereas in Alabama during the same school year the period of employment ranged from six months in ten counties to eight, ten, and twelve months in others. Sometimes the period of employment coincides exactly with the length of the school term in the county; more usually it is longer by one or two months so that the supervisor can engage in preliminary work before school opens in the fall of the year, and continue with conferences and visits to homes after the schools have closed in late spring or early summer.

For the Jeanes Teacher the number of months for which she is employed is important because her salary, like that of many American teachers, is on a monthly basis, and she is paid only for the number of months of her engagement. This monthly salary varies from county to county, sometimes because of differences in the number of schools to be supervised, but more usually because of differences in the amounts raised from public funds to supplement the contribution made by the Jeanes Trustees. As is to be expected, most salaries today are higher than the $40 a month which was paid to Virginia Randolph in the first year of her engagement, and in a normal year the rate of pay would now vary from $70 to $120 a month. Hard times have brought reductions in these salaries, as in many others, and another less noticeable economy which has proved equally trying for the Jeanes Teacher has been the cessation of the contribution formerly made by many counties towards her travelling expenses. In several cases which came to my notice, and which were no doubt typical of others, a great part of the Supervisor's salary was being absorbed by heavy travelling expenses, and as she also had to provide her own automobile and keep it in repair she was at times faced with rather difficult financial problems.[7] A few counties have refrained from economizing in this way, and it is to be hoped that the travelling allowances formerly made by others will shortly be restored.

Thirdly, the reader should know something of the conditions prevailing in the rural schools which the Jeanes Teacher visits and the quality of the teachers whom she tries to advise and help. Statistics are useful in that they enable us to compare the public school systems of various states in respect to certain measurable characteristics,[8] but they fail to convey an idea of the wide variations which are to be seen as the traveller moves from county to county. Here he will find a progressive county with a high proportion of Rosenwald schools, there a county with almost all its schools housed in churches, lodge halls, or other buildings in no way adapted for the accommodation of children. In one

---

[7] It is noticeable that married Jeanes Teachers whose husbands are in regular employment are usually less troubled in this way.
[8] See Appendix D, p. 141, for a few illustrative statistics.

THE JEANES TEACHER AT WORK 77

community the school building, whether old or new, will be found in decent repair and well cared for, in another the building will show every sign of local indifference and neglect, even of wilful destruction. In one school the pupils will be comfortably housed, carefully classified and reasonably well taught; in another the building will be overcrowded, and because of irregular attendance and poor teaching a large number of over-age pupils will be found in the lower grades. Of teaching equipment there will in some cases be a reasonable sufficiency; often, however, there may be little or none. In the words of an American observer: "To the visitor colored schools seem not a system but a series of incidents: bizarre, heroic, pathetic, romantic." [9]

And what of the teachers in these schools? Once again the visitor finds unexpected differences in their qualifications and suitability for teaching. A study published by the Julius Rosenwald Fund in 1931 shows that of a Negro teaching force numbering 47,426 in fifteen Southern States, 58 per cent (27,561) had less than the two years beyond high school which is usually regarded as the minimum preparation for teaching in elementary schools, while no less than 38.7 per cent (18,130) had not completed a full high school course.[10] But such statistics, though useful, must be interpreted with caution and may profitably be supplemented by the observations of the American writer quoted above, based on a wide knowledge of Negro schools.

[9] Edwin R. Embree, *Brown America*, p. 126.
[10] Fred. McCuistion, *The South's Negro Teaching Force*, pp. 17-20.

The average modern teacher will hold a certificate which proclaims her graduation from high school, although this may be anything from a modern, well-equipped, and accredited secondary institution with seventy teachers, to a school where three distraught women are handling all grades from the first through the twelfth. The teacher may get a salary of $25 a month for a five-month term, or $30 a month for four months or even three; while in an adjoining county a sister teacher may receive as much as $110 a month for nine months, and another in a nearby city may get an annual salary of $1750. In some instances the teacher may hold no certificate at all, or perhaps be using her sister's, as investigators found five teachers doing in one county. Or the teacher may hold a certificate based on a high school diploma which was given out gratis by the county superintendent in an effort to raise the rating of his staff.

Tests recently given to hundreds of teachers of these rural schools brought in an average score equivalent by national standards to that of a seventh-grade child. The teacher lives in some cases as far as five miles from the school, and often pays from $10 to $15 of her meagre monthly stipend for lodging and board. She is usually the product of a short school-term, poor teachers and low standards; her presence in the schoolroom perpetuates a vicious circle, relieved only by a resourcefulness and native wit that almost always bring in a few bright rays to an otherwise intolerable system.[11]

It is to such a miscellany of schools and teachers that the Jeanes Supervisors are called upon to minister, and the reader will by this time realize that their task is by

---

[11] Embree, *Brown America*, pp. 130-31.

THE JEANES TEACHER AT WORK 79

no means easy. The most complete record of the various ways in which they have attempted to carry out their duties is to be found in their monthly reports to State Agents for Negro Schools and to the Jeanes Trustees, and a few selections from reports for recent years will be of interest. The first is an extract from a typical report for September, the opening month of the school session.

From the 1st of Sept. through the 9th I visited homes and made a general visit to all schools trying to get ready for the opening Sept. 13th. . . . The month was spent helping teachers organize, filling out health cards, making daily programs and where there were new teachers, spending a whole day helping them to organize. In the afternoon we would visit the homes of patrons who would keep the largest out of school to gather crop and show them the importance of children coming the day school opens and met with splendid results.[12]

As the school year wears on, the activities of the Supervisor become more varied, and the following report for the month of January is typical of many others. The Supervisor in question reported that during the month she had visited 18 of the 28 schools and 24 of the 33 teachers in her district. In addition to these visits she had organized two group meetings for teachers, attended fifteen League meetings,[13] and paid eight visits to

---

[12] This and subsequent extracts are from Monthly Reports by Supervisors to the Jeanes Trustees.
[13] Meetings of local clubs or associations, often formed on the initiative of the Jeanes Teacher to stimulate public interest in and organize support for the school, or for community activities of various kinds.

homes. Here is a copy of her diary for the month, during which, incidentally, she had travelled 628 miles.

Date	School Community	Work done
1st	New Year	
2nd	Ch—	Visited Homes. Parents League Meeting.
3rd	D—	On official business.
4th	Ch—	Sent out circulars for group.
5th (Saturday)	Office	Work at home and in Superintendent's Office.
6th (Sunday)	Ch—	I address Young People's Meeting.
7th	R—	Health Talk. Class Supervision.
8th	B—	Health Talk. Class Supervision.
9th	H—	Conducted Classes in Group Work.
10th	Sh—	Conference with Parents. Class Inspection.
11th	St—	Supervised Class Work.
12th (Saturday)	Ch—	Conference with Teachers.
13th (Sunday)	Ch—	Church Services. Class Group.
14th	A—	Special request. Inspect building.
15th	P—	Collection of Xmas Seals. Class Supervision.
16th	R—	Special request. Inspect building.
17th	Sch—	Class Supervision.
18th	G—	Health Talk. Introduce National Negro History Week.
19th (Saturday)	R—	Group Meeting of Teachers.
20th (Sunday)	Ch—	Services at Church.
21st	H—	Health Talk. Collection of Stamps.
22nd	Illness at Home	
23rd	H— G—	Class Supervision. Collected Stamp Money.
24th	H—	Class Work. Health Talk.
25th	Ch—	Talk on National Negro History.
26th (Saturday)	Office	Corresponding with Teachers.
27th (Sunday)	Ch—	Church Service.
28th	L—	Plans with new Teacher.
29th	R—	Class Work. Supervised Health.
30th	T—	National Negro History Week.
31st	Conference with Miss C—	

The Jeanes Teacher, 1934

The Jeanes Teacher visits a rural school, February, 1934

THE JEANES TEACHER AT WORK 81

It is hardly necessary for our present purpose to reproduce in full similar reports from other Supervisors.[14] Many of the activities to which the writer of the above report refers are common to all Jeanes Teachers, and it will probably be more illuminating to add a few notes from other monthly reports in order to show how the emphasis may differ from time to time and from Supervisor to Supervisor. Here for example are several extracts from a batch of reports for the month of December, some of them with a seasonal flavour.

(a) Visited ten schools and communities. Most work done this month was study and training in menu making, cooking, sewing and table manners: distributing malaria blanks and Christmas seals among the schools. Gave Christmas presents to twenty-two children. Conducted two Christmas programs. Raised $24.25 for Church.

Improvement in school buildings and grounds: G—School; playground laid off and cleaned. Basket ball, volley ball and net bought. C—School: Basket ball court made, yard cleaned. L—School: Boys' basket ball court made, girls' improved. C-L—School: Schoolroom equipped with twenty-two desks, walls papered. St. M—School: Teacher's desk and chair bought. Plans made for the Annual Girls' Day Program.

(b) Twelve schools visited and Educational Test completed for this quarter and most of the papers graded. Talked on good manners and right conduct in each school. Much interest shown in preparing Christ-

[14] Several monthly reports from Jeanes Supervisors are reproduced in full in Lance Jones, *op. cit.*, pp. 141-46.

mas boxes, planning Christmas dinners, candy making, special decoration and general clean up for the holidays. Ten pairs of stockings, twelve under-garments, five dresses and more than three dollars spent for candy and fruit for the needy children.

Mt. O—. Three-teacher Rosenwald building completed and dedicated. A seven-room teacherage completed at F—. Contract let for Mt. M— School.

As the old year passed into history it left the schools on the upward trend to success. Ninety dollars raised this month.

(c) Seventy-six dollars has been raised this month from entertainments, style shows and movies in the school. Four beeves have been butchered and canned in S . . . and S . . . communities. . . . A part of the month was spent in assisting the Health Nurse. The children were weighed and heights taken in ten different schools.

(d) Up until now I have put special stress on sanitation and I am pleased to say that some of the schools have taken to the matter very attentively and were very consistent in the work. Yet I am sorry to say that some have failed to get the idea of sanitation as I think they should in having school pride. Therefore I will appreciate any advice by any Jeanes Supervisor or any Supervisor.

(e) G— School has already started improving their campus, that is they have made walks and planted rose bushes. Their P.T.A.[15] is also a live wire. If we had P.T.A.'s in all communities like this and a few others we could do more effective work. . . .

The last few weeks of the school session are frequently

[15] Parent-Teacher Association.

THE JEANES TEACHER AT WORK 83

devoted by the Jeanes Teacher to helping school principals arrange programmes for the commencement exercises with which every school in the United States marks the close of the year's work and the graduation of another batch of scholars.[16] Much time and energy are absorbed in this way, and if the school also stages an exhibition of pupils' work the Supervisor assists in its preparation. If she is ambitious she may go further and organize a county-wide rally in the form of a Field Day, with an exhibit of work from the schools in her area. The publicity value of both the smaller and the larger gathering is fully appreciated by the enthusiastic Supervisor. In friendly talks with school patrons or in the public speeches which she is invariably called upon to make, she seeks to arouse interest in her latest community project—home improvement, a health campaign, food raising, the building of a new school or the repairing of the old one—and the numbers who listen to her, or hear of her appeal indirectly, may often be considerable. Witness, for example, an entry in Virginia Randolph's diary for May 20th, "This week was known as Exhibit Week. We registered 2,684 people besides many children whose names we did not take. Field Day was well attended."

[16] Sometimes the programme is given a special emphasis, as is well illustrated by the following example: 1. Music. 2. Invocation. 3. Learning to Sew. 4. Learning to Cook. 5. Music. 6. A young Printer. 7. Learning to make Baskets. 8. Industrial Address. 9. A young Housekeeper. 10. Flowers in the Front Yard. 11. Music. 12. Learning to raise chickens. 13. Learning to mend shoes. 14. A young Carpenter. 15. Music. 16. Benediction. The industrial items were by children, the religious exercises by local ministers.

84 THE JEANES TEACHER

A second method of ascertaining how the Jeanes Teacher does her work is to go out with her, not to see special schools, but to share as a spectator in the routine of an ordinary day. It has been my privilege to be allowed to do this on several occasions, and so to supplement the knowledge gained in other ways. To see these women in personal contact with parents, teachers, and children gives a new meaning to the printed record of their activities, and an insight into their personalities which it would be difficult otherwise to obtain. Here, for example, is a brief summary of the visits made on one such day, lasting from about 8:30 in the morning to 3 o'clock in the afternoon and involving a journey of fifty to sixty miles by automobile over highroad and by-road. The summary is in note form for the sake of brevity.

(1) One-room, one-teacher school in poorly kept cabin rented from nearby householder to whom we spoke. Eleven pupils of all ages present, rough plank benches, no facilities for writing, few books.

Supervisor tested multiplication tables with homemade test cards, and explained to teacher (a young woman) how these could be made.

(2) School in church vestry, long narrow room totally unsuitable. One teacher, a man aged about 45 yrs. 40 pupils on roll, about 20 present, oldest boys out gathering firewood for school stove.

Supervisor tested reading from school books and from books of her own. Principal full of excuses for poor performance, resented Supervisor's kindly admonition about fuel gathering during school hours, and suggested

Assembling for a County Field Day

County Field Day: part of exhibit of industrial work

that boys would not learn much if they were in school!

(3) One-room, two-teacher school by railroad track. Building old, but in fair condition and well kept. Teachers (young women) both keen about school work and anxious to tell Supervisor about a Parents Rally which was to take place a few days later. Supervisor discussed plans for this, gave a short test in mental arithmetic to older pupils, and spoke to whole school about George Washington, whose birthday they had recently commemorated.

(4) One-room school, one teacher, a middle-aged woman. Sixty children on roll, about 25 present. Building new and substantial, but unfinished and very draughty. Teacher struggling hard (and with some success) to teach reading on modern lines.

Supervisor tested reading in several grades, and promised to lend teacher a printing set to make reading charts and flash cards. A mother present, listening to lessons with children: Supervisor spoke a friendly word to her.

(5) Two-room, two-teacher school, 100 pupils on roll, about 60 in attendance. Here the principal and assistant teacher, both women 35 to 40 years of age, were obviously not on friendly terms, and each had a special private word for the Supervisor's ear. She tactfully attempted to smooth away difficulties, and tested the work in each room before leaving.

All the buildings were of wood, as is usual in the South, and of reasonable size. In none of the schools visited did I see any sign of systematic industrial teaching, although in some cases the children had been trained to clean the schoolroom and keep the campus tidy. In every school the Supervisor examined the attendance registers (in one school the register was missing), and explained carefully to the children the importance of regular attendance, not only as a means of ensuring progress in their studies, but as an inducement to the authorities to keep open the school for a longer period. Such indeed was the main purpose of this particular round of calls, and accounted both for the number of schools visited and for the relatively short time spent in each. As a rule the Supervisor confines her attention to two or three schools a day and concentrates on the special problems of each.

Such records of visits to rural schools in the poorer and more backward sections of the South bring out clearly the need for sympathetic supervision. But because conditions vary so much a few details have been added of visits to other schools with Jeanes Teachers, or to schools in which Jeanes Teachers were already at work when I arrived. Again for the sake of brevity the details are given in note form.

(1) One-room, one-teacher school. Found building empty. Supervisor learned from neighbour that teacher had been to school but had left as no children appeared. Measles in community the possible explanation. Building in poor condition, no fasteners on door or on window shutters; benches frequently broken by marauders, no other furniture.

(2) Four-room, two-teacher school; building dilapidated but clean, two rooms only fit for use. Supervisor discussed class work at length with both teachers (one a young and the other a middle-aged woman) and tested reading in lower grades with flash cards. Results fair.

THE JEANES TEACHER AT WORK 87

Some drawing, paper-cutting and simple handwork. Teachers running school as a "pay-school" as the public funds were exhausted at the end of the previous month.

(3) Rosenwald School, brick, four rooms, four teachers, principal a man. Supervisor tested work in all classes; in principal's class and lowest class response poor, in other classes fair. Principal obviously thought himself superior to Jeanes Teacher; teacher of lowest grade an indolent young woman completely indifferent to excellent suggestions offered by Supervisor. Two remaining teachers welcomed advice and Supervisor commended their work.

(4) Rosenwald School, three rooms, three teachers, 140 children on roll, 85 in average attendance. Jeanes Supervisor busy preparing exhibit of sewing for Parents Day—garments and other simple but useful pieces of needlework. She explained that she herself taught the sewing at this school and at three others—one day a week at each—and that in one school she taught it to both boys and girls. No other organized industrial teaching, but teachers had trained children to keep the schoolroom clean and tidy.

(5) Two-room school, two women teachers, one young, one middle-aged. Building in good repair but not new: walls bright with posters and with specimens of class work. Supervisor examined the time table and work record of each teacher (which were carefully and neatly kept), tested reading and arithmetic, discussed difficulties of teaching arithmetic with assistant teacher, and a few general questions with the principal. Lower grades had completed a "farm project" and a model farm stood on a table in the room: questions showed that they had learnt a great deal from the project. Health Examination in progress, the Health Visitor

occupying the small room used for simple industrial teaching.

(6) Three-teacher school, about 100 children on roll, accommodated partly in a church and partly in a one-room frame building near by. Supervisor enquired about health teaching, singing and games, each of which she had recently been emphasising in her district. Tested each grade in the subject being taught at the time—results satisfactory. Knowledge of formal English Grammar in Grade 4 exceptionally accurate. A bright happy group of children; teachers (all women) exceptionally alert, clean and tidy.

Notes of similar visits could be multiplied and expanded but enough has been said to illustrate the various ways in which Jeanes Teachers are attempting to improve the schools under their care. The demands upon them are heavy, and they need much tact and patience as well as energy to carry them through their daily round of visits. Dr. Dillard once spoke of them as "carrying on day by day appointed tasks of helpfulness and encouragement" and it is in such a spirit that they come to the rural school. We cannot wonder therefore that they are among its most welcome visitors.

VII

The Jeanes Work
Adaptation and Experiment

The details given in the preceding chapter will have shown that the Jeanes Teacher today undertakes many tasks which did not concern the pioneers of the first ten or twelve years, and a comparison of summaries prepared by State Agents for Negro Schools brings out this fact still more clearly. Two such summaries are printed as an Appendix;[1] the first is for Virginia and the session 1912-13, the second for Louisiana and the session 1932-33. A comparison of these summaries, separated by an interval of twenty years, shows that while the old problems—improvement of school buildings and grounds, extension of terms, raising money for school equipment and teaching materials—have still to be faced, they no longer predominate. The Supervisor now spends much time helping teachers plan their work and improve their methods of teaching, sometimes by holding faculty meetings, at other times by giving demonstration lessons. During the session she may con-

[1] Appendix B, pp. 133-37.

duct several Teachers' Institutes for the whole county, at which problems of school organization and teaching method are discussed, and plans are laid for special events such as a County Field Day, a County-wide Literary Contest, a Negro History Week, or a Health Week. Visits to schools and homes figure in all reports, supplemented to an increasing degree in the later reports by meetings organized for groups of people—Parent-Teacher Associations, Mothers' Clubs, Canning Clubs, and the like. In these later reports, too, conferences with individuals appear more frequently—occasional conferences, for example, with the State Agent, more frequent conferences with the County Superintendent; conferences, too, as need arises, with the Home Demonstration Agent, the Health Nurse, or other state workers whose duties bring them from time to time into the county, and to whom the Jeanes Supervisor can often be of very great assistance. Finally, these varied activities necessitate an increasing amount of clerical work, such as the preparation of materials for lessons and conferences, the completing of official forms and reports, as well as correspondence with teachers and with the State Education Department. Indeed in some cases office work seems to absorb an undue proportion of the Supervisor's time.

Increasing variety and a marked change in emphasis therefore are noteworthy characteristics of the activities of Jeanes Supervisors of the present day as compared with those of their predecessors. Further confirmation of this changed and changing emphasis may readily be obtained by asking any group of Supervisors to set down

ADAPTATION AND EXPERIMENT 91

what they consider to be the main purpose of their work. Of fourteen Supervisors who did this at my request, twelve gave as their principal aims the improvement of class instruction, and the improvement of school conditions, particularly in the matter of sanitation and health. To these they added a few others—two Supervisors wished to develop industrial training, two to improve homes, two to bring about better race relations. The remainder merely amplified their earlier statements by specifying either school subjects or school conditions to which they wished to devote particular attention.[2] Individual Supervisors to whom I addressed a similar question usually returned much the same answer, and many who told me of their plans for the future incidentally showed that they were out to emphasize much the same aspects of their work. There can be little doubt therefore that many (probably most) Jeanes Teachers today consider that their main purpose is to supervise and improve classroom instruction in the ordinary school subjects, and that the teaching of industrial subjects, an outstanding interest of the earlier Supervisors, has fallen into the background. Indeed, by many it is entirely neglected.

An interesting comment on the present position is provided by a recent survey of Negro elementary schools, in which, after a summary of Jeanes work under four heads—the preparing of yearly plans for classroom instruction, the improvement of classroom teaching, the

---

[2] The answers of two Supervisors were so delightfully eloquent and vague as to defy classification.

use of county-wide examinations, score cards and similar devices in order to improve instruction, and the betterment of school and community conditions—there follows the criticism that "Supervisors are not stressing the supervision of instruction as much as is needed, nor so definitely as some other phases of their work. This means that the supervision of instruction is a neglected item in the rural school for Negroes." [3]

Clearly an explanation is called for. Supervisors who for the most part are anxious to encourage better methods of classroom instruction are nevertheless being criticized for lack of attention to this very thing! And if the criticism is justifiable, as it seems to be, what are the reasons for the alleged neglect? In the case of a few of the older teachers who are still genuinely interested in the teaching of industrial subjects, the reason simply is that they cling tenaciously to the old ways—sometimes, it must be admitted, because the inadequacy of their early education makes it difficult for them to take to the new. More usually, however, the explanation is to be found in the heavy demands which other duties are making upon Jeanes Teachers in many counties. They are expected to be not merely Supervisors of classroom instruction and community workers, but to an increasing extent administrative officers. In fact there are areas in which the Jeanes Teacher has virtually become the administrative assistant of the County Superintendent of Schools. This may be a convenient arrangement but

[3] *A Critical Survey of the Negro Elementary School (Journal of Negro Education*, Yearbook No. I, July, 1932), p. 237.

County Field Day: physical exercises

County Field Day: Maypole dancing

ADAPTATION AND EXPERIMENT 93

may not therefore be wholly commendable. Such, for example, is the judgment of a recent observer who after noting that "there seemed to be tendency on the part of some superintendents to unburden themselves of the worry of Negro schools by turning them over to a Negro supervisor," added "If the supervisor is merely a pretext for the superintendent's neglect of his Negro schools, the schools may be worse off for the supervisor's presence."[4] This is a hard saying, but it is none the less true.

Of the administrative duties which fall to the Jeanes Teacher that of reporting to County Superintendents and School Trustees on the suitability of candidates for appointment as teachers in small rural schools is probably the most important. Not many Supervisors are consulted in this way; those who are would seem to be in an exceptionally favourable position to bring about such improvements in rural schools as they may desire. But the difficulties with which they have to contend are many. The poorer and more educationally needy the school, the lower the salary offered is likely to be, and the more discouraging the physical conditions; in many Southern States standards of certification are lower for Negro than for white teachers; the quality of even those teachers who measure up to official standards is often very unsatisfactory; appointments are in the hands of school trustees and are for one school session only; teachers of low qualifications who are in favour with

[4] Clark Foreman, *Environmental Factors in Negro Elementary Education*, p. 32.

the school trustees and with the leading people of the locality, white and coloured, acquire a vested interest in their jobs and cannot be removed; appointments, in some cases, are obtained and held by gifts to trustees in money or in kind, and even in other and less reprehensible ways the Supervisor may be deterred from recommending the appointment of more competent teachers. Thus, the genial friendly teacher of a rural school may be an excellent agent in the raising of money for much needed improvements, but the poorest of teachers in the classroom, a situation which places the Jeanes Teacher in a dilemma. Only in states where there exists some degree of central control in education can the knowledge and experience of the Jeanes Supervisor be made full use of in this matter of securing more efficient teachers for rural schools, and even in such a case she may still meet with difficulties. If the area (state or county) is one in which appointment on merit is a recent innovation she is liable to be suspected of favouritism, and in many a county even her own tenure of appointment may be precarious.[5]

Another task which most Jeanes Teachers are called upon to undertake is that of acting as attendance officers for the counties to which they are attached. There are certain obvious advantages in having them do this work. It necessitates (or should necessitate) regular visits to

---

[5] The lack of continuity in the service of teachers is a serious drawback to Negro education. Thus the average tenure of teachers in Negro elementary schools is estimated to be less than two years, and within a recent three-year period there were no less than sixty changes in Jeanes Teachers in the state of Georgia.

ADAPTATION AND EXPERIMENT 95

all schools, it should take the Jeanes Teacher into homes, and enable her to judge how far the school is making any impression on the great mass of illiteracy and ignorance which still exists. But attendance laws are rarely if ever enforced; attendance registers, either through ignorance, wilful neglect, or misrepresentation, are often grossly misleading. Parents and employers suit their own convenience, and children their own pleasure as to attendance or non-attendance at school, with the result that such attraction as the school itself can exert remains the only means whereby regular attendance may be secured.[6] When through the incompetence and inertness of the teacher this attraction fails, the Supervisor is indeed helpless. The fact that in spite of these great handicaps she has succeeded in arousing so many rural teachers to co-operate with her and to increase year by year both the enrolment and the actual attendance at rural elementary schools is a testimony, if any were needed, to her devoted labour and personal influence in the community. She can do much by direct appeal to teachers and children, but probably her most effective work in the cause of regular attendance at school is done during those home visits which still figure

[6] Statistics show that one million Negro children of school age are not enrolled in any school, and that the average daily attendance only represents about 75 per cent of those actually enrolled. Agricultural work or other employment probably accounts for one-half the absences from rural schools. Other causes listed by the principal teacher of one large school as a basis for analysing absences were: Ill-health, Sickness in family, Accident, Marriage, Death, Mental Condition, Over age, Moved house, Lack of clothing, shoes, or books, Committed to Institution, Movies.

in most reports, and which keep her in touch with the life and needs of her people.

The third kind of activity of an administrative or semi-administrative character undertaken by the Jeanes Teacher is the organizing of county-wide events such as a County Field Day, which, as we have already noted, have considerable publicity value. As many schools as possible must participate either in the programme of exercises for the day, or in the exhibit of school work which forms one of the major attractions. As great a variety of work as possible must be selected and assembled at some central point, including, for example, written exercises from the grades, plain and fancy needlework, ingeniously made articles of wood and raffia, baskets of pine needles and of honeysuckle, shuck mats, garden produce, together with exhibits representing every kind of group activity. One exhibition which I saw included articles made by parents (rugs and quilts), with the result that the interest of the community was still more effectively aroused. Prizes are sometimes given to the more successful schools for their exhibits, and the Supervisor usually contrives to provide for this purpose articles which can be used by the teachers or children in their school work—a few books, maps, pictures, or a much coveted printing set.

In assembling and arranging exhibits and in planning the programme for the day the wise Jeanes Teacher enlists the help of a small committee, but when the actual day arrives she has to act as "Mistress of Ceremonies," and right well she usually does it. It is no light

Exhibit of industrial work: chair caning

Exhibit of needlework

ADAPTATION AND EXPERIMENT 97

task. She must be tactful, for local men of note (such as school trustees and ministers of religion), will be present, possibly also the County Superintendent of Schools or even the State Agent for Negro Schools, and as many of these gentlemen as possible must be allowed to take part in the day's proceedings. She must be patient, for the gathering will include coloured people of all ages from every part of the county; they will almost certainly arrive late, engage in incessant friendly chatter during the proceedings, sing spirituals without regard to the passing of time, interpret all intervals generously, and stroll in and out of the assembly as they feel inclined. She must be firm, and use all her native forcefulness and wit if she is to control such a heterogeneous assembly. But they are a good-humoured and kindly crowd, and once she can catch and hold their attention she is sure of a sympathetic hearing. Indeed there is something of a revivalist atmosphere about these gatherings when the Jeanes Teacher, full of zeal for school or community improvement, touches the pride and arouses the enthusiasm of her audience. The concrete results may seem small, but the inspiration derived from these meetings has been the force behind many a local effort towards school improvement. Without leaders whom they could understand the coloured people would have remained uninformed and undirected, and as leaders in the cause of education and social improvement the Jeanes Teachers have played their part well.[7]

[7] Compare with the above description Jackson Davis's account of a Field Day and County Exhibit printed as Appendix C, pp. 138-39.

Often, too, these public assemblies may have a value of rather a different kind. This was so in the case of one county-wide rally at which I was present. Here for the first time Negroes were being permitted to hold a public meeting in the county courthouse, and a few of the leading white citizens were enjoying what was for most of them the novel experience of participating in a gathering organized by and for coloured people. Everyone was feeling a little strange and rather nervous, but the day's proceedings passed off reasonably well, and when the long drawn out programme came to an end the community had taken another modest step forward in the direction of a better understanding between white and coloured people. Those of my readers who are familiar with social conditions in the more backward counties of the rural South will realize that to carry through successfully the first of such organized efforts is no mean achievement.

When we turn to examine the efforts which Supervisors are making to improve the teaching in rural schools we find that this side of their work is but a more modest attempt to do for Negro schools what progressive elementary school Supervisors throughout the United States are doing for white schools. But even so, a few illustrations of the methods employed by the more efficient Jeanes Teachers will be advisable. Consider, for example, the problems of organization which face the newly appointed teacher of a one-room school enrolling from fifty to one hundred pupils of all ages, sizes, and degrees of attainment, problems which would

ADAPTATION AND EXPERIMENT

tax the ingenuity and resourcefulness of the most experienced teacher. Here the Supervisor offers welcome help, and by the use of standard tests in the basic subjects of reading and arithmetic, grades and classifies the pupils sufficiently for the regular teacher to make some kind of start. Or the problem may be that of teaching reading to beginners of varied ages with only a few tattered and antiquated readers, and no aids of the kind so common in every decently equipped school. Again the Jeanes Teacher is at hand with home-made apparatus—letters, flash cards, reading charts, and even simple story books—any or all of which she may lend to the teacher for a few weeks and which she encourages her to copy. Possibly the problem to be tackled is the teaching of a particular subject, such as arithmetic, and it is necessary to work out a graded syllabus and methods of teaching. Once more the efficient Supervisor is ready, this time with a syllabus divided into units of work which ensure orderly progression by stages within the comprehension of both teacher and pupil. Finally, towards the end of the session, the Supervisor may give to the pupils in each grade tests in the principal school subjects in order to gauge their progress and stimulate or encourage the class teacher.

By the use of similar methods the up-to-date Jeanes Teacher who is desirous of maintaining and developing industrial activities as an essential element in school life assists the rural teacher to organize these subjects also. In Alabama, for example, there have been in use for several years some excellently planned unit courses in sewing, devised in the first place by the State Supervisor of Jeanes Teachers, and passed on to the rural schools by County Supervisors. So too, in other areas, Jeanes Teachers are showing how the curriculum of the small rural school may be enriched by the introduction of systematic teaching in such subjects as physical education and games, both very much needed in coloured schools.

Visits to schools for the purpose of disseminating ideas and distributing teaching materials are supplemented by group meetings for teachers from a number of neighbouring schools, or by "Institutes" for the whole county. These usually take place on Saturdays, and include both morning and afternoon sessions. Sometimes they are held on a school day in a centrally located school in order that the programme may include demonstration teaching, in which case the schools of visiting teachers are closed, and they have no excuse for non-attendance. At one group meeting which I attended twenty-seven visiting teachers were present (seven men and twenty women), and the morning session was devoted to observing lessons by the regular teachers of the school—first grade arithmetic, beginners' reading, second grade language, a second grade number lesson to illustrate the use of "dramatic" or practical methods, and last of all, a seventh grade arithmetic lesson. The visiting teachers had been provided by the Supervisor in charge with a few leading questions to guide them in their observations, and these also furnished the main headings under which the morning's

Assembling for a teachers' institute

A group of Jeanes Supervisors, 1917

ADAPTATION AND EXPERIMENT 101

lessons were discussed during the afternoon session. This discussion was tactfully guided by the Supervisor, who saw that the strong and weak points in each lesson received appropriate emphasis, and as opportunity arose, offered hints about alternative methods and suitable materials. The meeting ended with a discussion of arrangements for forthcoming school commencements, and with much friendly talk which must have been very welcome to teachers from isolated one-room schools. Indeed a well-organized conference of this kind is one of the very best ways in which the Jeanes Teacher can spread her ideas and awaken in the rural teacher a desire to improve her methods of teaching.

The most alert and inventive of Supervisors, however, needs occasional stimulus and refreshment. State Agents realize this and organize conferences for Jeanes Teachers in their areas, while Dr. Dillard and his successor, Arthur D. Wright, from time to time arrange similar meetings for Supervisors from a wider area.[8] Jeanes Teachers have also been encouraged and assisted to attend summer schools in order to improve either their academic or their professional qualifications; most of them eagerly avail themselves of such opportunities, and speak with enthusiasm of the experience and inspiration so gained. Usually the courses they complete at summer schools are of a conventional type, but in recent years

---

[8] The largest assembly of Jeanes Teachers ever held took place in 1931 when 313 Supervisors from 310 counties attended a conference at Tuskegee Institute. The occasion was an exceptional one, for the main purpose of the gathering was to make a presentation from the Jeanes Supervisors to Dr. Dillard on his retirement.

efforts have been made to deal specifically with the needs and problems of the Negro rural school, and, with the encouragement and financial assistance of the Jeanes Trustees and the General Education Board, experiments are being tried which may prove to be of very real significance, and in which Jeanes Teachers are likely to play an important part.

The cause of these experiments is to be found in the dissatisfaction which has long been felt with the methods of teaching prevalent in one-teacher rural schools, and the failure to effect any real improvement. For some years most American educators seem to have thought that such schools could and should be eliminated by a process of consolidation, but this consolidation is not likely to be achieved during the lifetime of the present generation, nor is everyone now quite sure that the small school is so hopeless an educational adventure as was once thought to be the case.[9] A number of teacher-training institutions have in the past tried to familiarize their students with rural school conditions—one of them has for some years used a neighbouring one-teacher school for demonstration purposes; another has set up a small two-room school on the campus, while at one time a third college arranged for its students to spend a few weeks in a rural school as part of their practice teaching. In most colleges, too, opportunity is given for the discussion of rural school problems, but these meth-

[9] In 1927 there were 22,494 Negro rural schools in the South. Of these 15,358 were one-teacher schools, and 4,523 were two-teacher schools. S. L. Smith, "Negro Schools in the South," article in *The Southern Workman*, Vol. LVI, No. 7 (July, 1927).

ADAPTATION AND EXPERIMENT 103

ods of approach do not seem to have brought about the improvement which might have been expected. For this reason the General Education Board in 1932 initiated experiments of a more fundamental character, and by special grants made possible the employment in a number of summer schools of skilled teachers able to conduct demonstrations of methods suitable for small rural schools. Of these experiments the one conducted by Atlanta University, in its 1933 summer school, will serve as an excellent example.

The underlying idea was very simple: it was that during the summer school organized by Atlanta University and its affiliated colleges (which incidentally is attended each year by many teachers from rural schools), there should be in operation a one-teacher school in a typical rural section of Georgia. The school chosen for the experiment was 17 miles distant from Atlanta, 45 children were enrolled for a special six-week session, and an average attendance of 38 secured. The school was open from Tuesday to Saturday in each of the six weeks, and from 8 A.M. to 2:30 P.M. each day. On Mondays the teacher in charge of the school met the students of the Rural Education group at Atlanta University, and on two days in each week the group went out to the school.

In essence the experiment was an attempt to demonstrate in a much more thoroughgoing fashion how the difficulties presented by the one-room one-teacher school might be attacked. Before school opened the teacher in charge acquainted herself with conditions in the community by a series of home visits. On the basis of the knowledge obtained by this and other means a preliminary classification of the children into grades was attempted. When school opened tests were given by the summer school instructor in psychology and his class in order to ascertain more precisely the attainments of each child in the basic subjects of reading and arithmetic, while on the second day of school the university physician and nurse made a careful physical examination of the pupils. These preliminaries over, the children were divided into three groups which thereafter formed the units for teaching purposes. By a careful co-ordination of subject matter, and by making practical projects (such as keeping house) the centre of interest whenever possible, the teacher contrived to keep the children in each group working together, and so avoided the almost chaotic conditions prevailing in most one-room rural schools, where an earnest but weary teacher may be seen vainly attempting to teach a little of every subject to every grade on every day. Lessons in certain subjects, such as music, civics, and health, were given to the whole school, and in every possible way the value of careful organization of school work was emphasized and convincingly demonstrated.

This was the more original side of the experiment, but not by any means its only value. For the teacher in charge, like the Jeanes Teachers whose work we have been describing, realized what a great help it would be to establish a close connection between the community and the school. She therefore arranged that parents and

A group of County Training School principals and Jeanes Teachers with officers of the Jeanes and Slater Funds, 1923

A group of Negro teachers

ADAPTATION AND EXPERIMENT 105

friends should meet at the school each Tuesday afternoon, sometimes to discuss school problems, sometimes for recreation, sometimes for a lecture or discussion—for example, on the value of home gardening, or improved methods of farming. The interest thus aroused in the school found practical expression when patrons helped to clear the campus, and undertook to make certain improvements in the building. Some white residents also became interested and helpful, and in a variety of ways the school was linked up more closely with the community, to their mutual benefit. "Little can be accomplished in six weeks' time," says a report on the experiment in the Spelman College magazine, "but in this case that little is extremely significant. A new key-note has been set for the community. There's an enthusiasm, a hopefulness, a faith that co-operation may result in accomplishment.... Everyone seemed in accord with the sentiment of one parent who said 'We's gwine ter climb de saplin wid yer 'twel it bends.' " [10]

Such a carefully planned experiment at a time when administrators and Supervisors were anxiously reconsidering the kindred problems of curriculum and teaching methods in rural schools could not fail to attract attention, and it was natural that this and similar experiments should come under discussion at two small but representative conferences which met in the spring

[10] *The Spelman Messenger*, August, 1933. The details are taken from this and from a fuller manuscript report by Miss Elizabeth T. Perry of the Spelman College Faculty, who conducted the experimental rural school, and discussed the experiment with me. Spelman College (for women) is one of the constituent colleges of Atlanta University.

of 1934 at Hampton and Tuskegee Institutes to consider the special problems of the smaller rural schools. One result of these conferences has been to confirm the value of the experiments at Atlanta and other summer schools, another to spread the knowledge of them widely throughout the South. It is here that the key position of the Jeanes Supervisor becomes of the greatest possible importance. Unless she has a keen appreciation of the need for better methods of classroom instruction, as well as the ability to understand and explain to others the methods now suggested, rural schools will not greatly benefit by these experiments, and without her help and continued encouragement the overworked and ill-equipped teacher of the one-room rural school can scarcely hope to achieve the desired results. The effectiveness of any gospel depends in great measure on the faithfulness, zeal, and intelligence of its interpreters, and to this the missionary work of the Jeanes Teachers is no exception.

For today, as in the early years of their work, the Jeanes Teachers are the South's most effective missionaries in the cause of education. There have been changes in the gospel they have been called upon to preach—twenty-five years ago it was a gospel of work with the hands, today school organization and method take prior place in their message; there have been heavy increases in the demands made upon them, with an inevitable loss of spontaneity and initiative; there has been a wider dissemination among them of modern conceptions and modern methods of education with a resulting approxi-

ADAPTATION AND EXPERIMENT

mation to common standards; but these changes have in no way diminished their zeal for the cause they have at heart. In the uphill climb of the Negro rural school they have ungrudgingly given help and encouragement to the lonely rural teacher, in the difficult times through which the schools are now passing they are spending themselves untiringly in efforts to keep schools open and bring such help as is available to their needy pupils, and in any forward movement which may take place in the years to come it will fall to them to be the advance guard. Their record suggests that they will not flinch from the challenge.

VIII

After Twenty-five Years

IN FEBRUARY, 1933, the Jeanes Trustees completed twenty-five years' administration of the fund placed at their disposal by Miss Anna T. Jeanes, and the earlier chapters of this study have shown how faithfully and wisely they have fulfilled their trust. It remains only to re-emphasize the salient features of the movement which has developed under their guidance, and to estimate the significance of changes which have taken place in recent years and are still in progress.

The outstanding characteristic of the Jeanes work has been its concentration on the needs of rural schools and rural communities. That this should be so was a necessity laid upon the Trustees by the terms of Miss Jeanes's benefaction. She had in mind "that great class of Negroes to whom the small rural and community schools are alone available," and desired that they should be helped through these schools to obtain "rudimentary education." To this end Jeanes Teachers have promoted schemes for the building or renovating of schools, visited homes in order to enlist the interest of parents and increase school attendance, fostered habits of personal cleanliness in children and adults by means of health talks, introduced better methods of teaching the usual school subjects, and thus have brought about a marked improvement in hundreds of rural schools. Critics from time to time have questioned the value of this or that activity, but the spirit in which the Jeanes Teachers have carried out their task has been beyond reproach, and would have been warmly commended by the practical-minded little lady whose sympathy and generosity made their work possible.

The many other activities which now devolve upon the Jeanes Teacher and which, for the sake of convenience, may be described as administrative, have also contributed to the development of rural education, and in particular to its better organization and greater efficiency. It is sometimes suggested that the benefits which accrue from them are not so much to the advantage of pupils in the small rural schools and dwellers in the surrounding rural communities as to the advantage of the whole school system and its administrative officers in particular. The criticism is not without force, inasmuch as efficiency in administration and in supervision may easily become ends in themselves, but in so far as they contribute (as they should) to the improvement of the individual school they may certainly be regarded as legitimate extensions of the Jeanes work, and not necessarily alien to the spirit of the trust. Indeed there can be few activities centering in the rural school and designed to educate the rural Negro which need be excluded, and the Jeanes Trustees realize that the possibilities of further experiment and expansion have by no means been exhausted. Nevertheless, while admitting the value of all that has been done, experienced observers are concerned lest the changes which have taken place in recent years should lead to an increasing neglect of principles which they regard as fundamental in rural education.

The ideal which such observers have in mind is well expressed by Dr. Dillard in a statement of policy made in the early days on behalf of the Jeanes Trustees, and quoted in an earlier chapter.[1] Briefly the ideal may be described as the linking of rural education to rural life. While welcoming every form of community activity which improves the physical conditions under which pupils are taught, and every effort to improve the quality of the teaching, these observers suggest that if the association of the school with its environment is to be of permanent value, other and more fundamental changes are needed. The curriculum should draw as much of its material as possible from the immediate surroundings, school activities should be related more nearly to the pupils' daily lives, and the school should be a centre not only for social gatherings to raise funds, but also for the continued education of adolescents and adults by means of co-operative and socially useful activities. It is essential that every child should learn to read, to write, and to perform a few simple calculations, but whereas these skills, if mechanically acquired, too frequently are lost for want of appropriate exercise,

[1] Pp. 67-68, *supra*.

they are far less likely to lapse if the pupil has acquired them as part of an interested, alert, and active response to his whole environment.

It is in this connection that the question of the so-called industrial subjects arises—surely a misleading designation if applied to such activities as can be included in the curriculum of a rural elementary school. Plain sewing, sometimes a little cooking, the making and repairing of simple utensils for school or for home, a little gardening, the making of baskets from pine needles or of shuck mats from maize straw, simple work in wool, paper or raffia, the cleaning and beautifying of the school and its surroundings—these were the activities introduced by the pioneer Jeanes Teachers and their immediate successors. Often, no doubt, they were unintelligently taught and of little educational value, but today in many rural schools nothing of the kind is attempted, and from many others such occupations are rapidly disappearing. Sometimes the Supervisor explains that time cannot be spared from the more legitimate activities of the school, an argument occasionally used also by Negro patrons, among whom there lingers a suspicion that to depart from a purely academic curriculum would be to admit racial inferiority. Sometimes the teacher of the rural school has neither the inclination nor the ability to plan and carry through a school programme of this more practical kind. Most frequently the omission is taken as a matter of course, and seems to arise from a widespread reaction against subjects of a vocational character, a realization that no vocational training of any importance can be given in the small rural elementary school, and a failure to perceive that practical activities are of great educational value in that they provide a simple and effective means of ensuring the all-round development of the individual child. Whatever the cause, it seems strange that in a country whose educators were quick to recognize the social and still more the educational importance of subjects and of methods which link together school and community, and among a group whose success in this direction has inspired similar efforts in other lands, reaction should have gone so far. It is, however, a hopeful sign that the summer school experiments to which we referred in the preceding chapter should aim at revising school curricula and teaching methods so as once again to bridge the gap between school and home. Only an education which does this can fit the "great class of Negroes to whom the small rural and community schools alone are available" for a fuller and more satisfying life.[2]

Not wholly unconnected with this failure to appreciate the educational value of the school environment is a change which is worth noting, but of which it is difficult to gauge the extent. Automobiles now make it possible for many Jeanes Teachers to live in towns, from which they drive out daily on their round of school visits; some of them, too, were born in towns, educated on conventional lines in town schools, have taught in

[2] The reader will find an interesting and suggestive discussion of Negro rural education along these lines in *The Reorganization and Redirection of Negro Education* (*Journal of Negro Education*, Yearbook No. V, July, 1936), Chaps. XII-XV.

AFTER TWENTY-FIVE YEARS 113

town schools, and, very naturally, are town-minded. It would be foolish to infer that all such teachers are therefore incapable of understanding the conditions of rural life or realizing the educational possibilities of a rural environment—Virginia Randolph herself has lived all her life in the city of Richmond—but it is perhaps not unreasonable to suggest that an increasing recruitment of Supervisors with neither experience of rural life nor of rural schools may hinder rather than help the present movement for the revitalizing of rural education.

A second characteristic of the Jeanes work and one which has become increasingly noticeable is its emphasis on school supervision—in the professional sense. Such supervision includes a wide range of duties, some administrative and some directed towards improving the teaching of the usual school subjects. Once again the change seems to be in accordance with the swing of educational opinion, and in spite of the excellent work they have accomplished in this field, Jeanes Supervisors have not moved fast enough in the desired direction for some of their critics. Several reasons for this have already been indicated, but one of them should perhaps be emphasized a little more—namely the fact that the Jeanes Teacher has become the "maid of all work" of the Negro school system. Her duties have always been varied and exacting, but it is not usually realized that the advent of the automobile has increased the demands made upon her, and also the physical strain of meeting them. The result at times is seen in haste and overpressure during the school session, not wholly compensated for by the length of the summer vacation. Even Supervisors who keep pace with their obligations cannot hope to discharge them all with equal thoroughness, and the temptation to perfunctoriness in carrying out the less interesting of their duties is very great. It is to their credit that so few succumb.

Again, in the early days of rural school supervision the Jeanes Teacher was not so much "maid of all work" as "Jack of all Trades," and was ready and eager to render any and every kind of service—indeed the versatility of some of the pioneers must have been remarkable. Today, however, the demands made upon her are not merely more numerous but also more exacting—in the matter of classroom supervision for example—and some reconsideration of her place in the educational and social life of the community is called for, lest by endeavouring still to remain "Jack of all Trades" she should end by becoming master of none.

A third characteristic of the Jeanes work has been the pioneer spirit in which it has been undertaken, and the willingness to explore and experiment which have hitherto made it so interesting and varied. But the busy bustling life of many Jeanes Teachers at the present time is apt to leave them very much at the mercy of circumstances, unable or disinclined to make and carry out continuously plans for school improvement other than those suggested to them. From being the inspirers of modest experiments they are in danger of becoming mere channels for conveying ideas to the schools. The introduction of new ideas is excellent and indeed essential to the revivifying of school curricula and teaching methods, but if in the process there should be a sacrifice of initiative and independent judgment on the part of those in immediate contact with the schools the loss to rural education will be great. There are more problems and possibilities in the conducting of a rural school than the mind of even the ablest administrator or Professor of Education can conceive, and it would be a misfortune if in their pardonable zeal to keep abreast of the times Jeanes Teachers should cease to make their own modest contribution to educational practice. Supervisors who have been well educated and carefully trained, who have to their credit years of successful experience as teachers in rural schools, and who are fitted by character and outlook for their work, are in a better position than almost anyone in the school system to try out ways and means of helping the one-teacher and two-teacher school.

The fourth characteristic of the Jeanes work to which it is desirable to draw attention is one to which only occasional reference has so far been made, but which is of profound significance. Jeanes Teachers, by reason of their varied activities, have been brought into contact with people of different classes and of both races, and by their earnest desire to render service, practically and unostentatiously, have inspired confidence and helped greatly towards a better understanding between white and coloured people in rural communities. The present tendency, however, seems to be towards a type of administrative specialization which devolves increasing responsibility for Negro schools upon the Jeanes Supervisor, with the possible result that, as the provision of public schools becomes more adequate and the need for local community effort less urgent, both Supervisor and schools may be separated more completely than ever from the public school system as a whole. It may be that we have here but another illustration of the increasing separation which is growing up between the races throughout the country, but from an educational standpoint the tendency is to be regretted, and should surely be avoided if at all possible. Consultation and exchange of ideas between the supervisory staffs for white and coloured schools should continue and be extended, and though the time of its fulfilment may be far distant, we may at least express the hope that some day rural teachers from white and Negro schools may meet in conference to discuss their common problems. Co-operation between the more intelligent and progressive members of both races along the lines of a common interest is the surest way to bring about mutual understanding and good will.

Finally, we must remind the reader of the essentially co-operative nature of every activity promoted by the Jeanes Trustees, and of the success which has attended their policy of acting at all times in association with the authorities responsible for public education. The evidence of their success is to be seen in the increasing measure of interest and financial support accorded to the Jeanes work, but gratifying though this may be, it is

AFTER TWENTY-FIVE YEARS 117

greatly to be regretted that only one state (Maryland) has so far been willing to take over the whole burden of supervising its Negro public schools.[3] Sometimes the delay seems to be due to scepticism about the value of supervision, or it may be that County Boards of Education are loth to relinquish a means of securing additional aid for schools which are never adequately provided for and sometimes starved. More often the localized character of educational administration and finance is the real difficulty. Counties vary as widely in their resources and administrative efficiency as in their zeal for education, and if the movement towards greater administrative centralization should make headway in the South it ought to result in a progressive equalization of advantages throughout each state. Such a development would make easier the transition to a system of supervision wholly organized and maintained by the respective states—the only solution which can be regarded as permanent and satisfactory.

It is unlikely that the next few years will see any marked change in the character of the Jeanes work. Efforts will continue with a view to extending rural school supervision throughout the South, the activities of the Jeanes Teacher will become more specialized, and an increasing emphasis will be placed on classroom instruc-

[3] For reasons of economy the North Carolina State Board of Education in 1933 required every Jeanes Teacher to carry a full load as school teacher or principal, and to do all Jeanes work before and after school hours, on Saturdays or during school vacations. Their salaries and expenses as Jeanes Teachers had to be met wholly by the Jeanes or other donated funds. It is to be hoped that this will prove to be only a temporary arrangement.

tion. A word or two about each of these possible developments may fittingly conclude this chapter.

In the first place there can be little doubt as to the need for the supervision of all Negro rural schools throughout the South, and if the Jeanes Trustees could somehow be provided with the necessary funds to extend their experiment to the counties where Negro schools are still uncared for in this way the extension would provide them with experience of very great value.[4] Twenty-five years' handling of the difficult problem of rural school supervision should make it possible to map out a programme of extension on lines suited to the ideas and conditions of the time, and to initiate a phase of the movement which, in its way, would be as significant as that which we have attempted to review. By the time this desirable extension had been achieved it might well be that public interest will have resulted in such an increased measure of public support that the Trustees could turn their attention to other aspects of rural education. Until then it would seem wise to continue the great experiment to which they have set their hands.

With this geographical expansion will go an increasing measure of concentration, and in some areas it is already becoming desirable and possible to delimit more precisely the work of the Jeanes Teacher. State Health

---

[4] Wright, *op. cit.*, p. 20, states that on April 1, 1933, there were 1110 counties in fourteen Southern States without Jeanes Teachers. He adds that, assuming a Supervisor to be unnecessary in counties with less than ten Negro teachers, there were still at that time 499 counties in which Jeanes Teachers were needed.

AFTER TWENTY-FIVE YEARS 119

and Welfare Services are coming into being, and with an increasing sense of responsibility on the part of the community are being extended to the Negro population. Thus the North Carolina State Board of Charities and Public Welfare in 1925 established a Division of Work among Negroes which initiated medical inspection of Negro schools, and also conducted a special investigation into the problem of school attendance in six counties of the state.[5] Welfare officers throughout the state regularly enquire into the causes of absence from school, and there is obviously in this arrangement a basis of co-operation which would relieve the Jeanes Supervisor of some of her present responsibilities. The arrangement, too, is a reasonable one, since absence from school is frequently due to ill-health or unsatisfactory home conditions.[6] Again in most states, Farm and Home Demonstrators have been at work for many years, and there are counties in which they co-operate willingly with the Jeanes Supervisor in organizing Farm and Home-Makers Clubs, or in less ambitious schemes designed to awaken the interest of children in rural schools. The ideal arrangement is seen at those few centres where a well-equipped school has become the headquarters of a team of County Agents, of whom the Jeanes Supervisor is one.[7] Under such an arrangement the Supervisor would concern herself primarily with

[5] North Carolina State Board of Charities and Public Welfare, *School Attendance in North Carolina: A Survey of Six Counties*, 1931.
[6] See footnote, p. 95.
[7] For example—Fort Valley School, Georgia, or Penn School, St. Helena Island, South Carolina.

improving the standard of education in rural schools, link school activities whenever possible with those of the home, and through the schools co-operate in various ways with her colleagues in special efforts on behalf of the whole community. It would be excellent if further experiments in organized team work could be initiated, centering, for example, on a few county training schools which have not lost touch with community life. Such experiments would more than repay the time and expense involved in setting them afoot and maintaining them for a period sufficient to show their real value.

The most recent form of specialisation by the Jeanes Teacher is an increasing concentration on classroom supervision; this is more particularly the case in those counties where a passable minimum of schoolroom accommodation has been provided, but is also noticeable in other and far less favourable circumstances. Curricula are being revised, the day's work more intelligently planned, methods of teaching overhauled. Much has been and will be accomplished by methods we have described elsewhere and which the Jeanes Supervisors can be trusted to continue and extend; the special problems of the small rural school will no doubt receive increasing attention also in normal schools and summer schools. But in the long run the success or failure of supervision must depend on the quality of the rural teacher, and here the Jeanes Supervisor can rarely exercise more than a very indirect influence. Higher standards of professional conduct and stricter administrative control are needed to eliminate the idle and careless teacher; high schools which teach fewer subjects well, and normal schools which build with equal thoroughness on this more stable foundation are essential; so too are County Boards of Education and County Superintendents who refuse to issue professional certificates of little or no value, and a public opinion which will no longer justify or condone in Negro public schools conditions not tolerated elsewhere. Until such changes in Southern educational policy and practice can be effected the labours of the Jeanes Supervisor, however earnest and well prepared she may be, will be robbed of their full effect, and when these changes have come to pass, as some day they surely must, a new phase in the history of rural school supervision will have begun.

IX

THE CHANGING SOUTH

THE TWENTY-FIVE years covered by this study have been eventful years for the South and have brought many changes. Industry has developed apace both above and below the Potomac, and the Southern Negro has flocked townward to swell the great coloured populations of New York, Chicago, Philadelphia, and Baltimore, or to find a home in the growing coloured sections of Washington, New Orleans, Birmingham, Atlanta, and many a lesser Southern city. In the North he could escape from many irksome restrictions; in the towns (North and South) he could hope to find more remunerative employment, a fuller social life, and, very probably, better schools for his children. Agriculture, once his sole occupation, now accounts for less than one-half of the Negroes gainfully employed. Manufacture, domestic service, mining, transport, trade, commerce and the professions all claim their quotas, and the social pattern of the Negro section in any large town is fast becoming a replica of the white community beside which it dwells. The percentage of Negroes in the rural South is steadily decreasing, and everywhere,

THE CHANGING SOUTH

North and South, the Negro is becoming increasingly race-conscious and proud of his achievement.[1]

His pride is legitimate, for he has travelled far since the days of slavery. He can point to banks and insurance companies which have weathered the financial storms of the past few years, to businesses, farms, and homes which his people own, to a Negro press, to singers, composers, painters, sculptors, men of letters, scientists, and physicians of his own race, to an increasing enrolment in every type of school and a continuous decline in illiteracy. It is an encouraging record although there is, unfortunately, another and less pleasing side to the picture. In Southern cities the Negro enjoys few public amenities; in Southern States he is denied the full protection of the law; his schools, though no longer ignored, fare badly in the allocation of public funds, while a restricted franchise and a system of voting by white primaries effectively exclude him from politics.[2] In spite of the remarkable progress the race has made, the Southern Negro still remains the most under-privileged group in the great American republic.

What the future may hold no one can safely predict. The recent economic depression has shown how insecure is the Negro's position in industry, for not only his more recently acquired occupations but his traditional employments also have been unhesitatingly taken

---

[1] For statistics of Negro population, etc., *see* Appendix D, pp. 140-41.
[2] The primary (Democratic or Republican) is the local association of party members which designates candidates for the smaller authorities and also delegates for the convention which selects candidates for the higher political offices.

from him by his white competitors.[3] Drastic reductions in cotton acreage have brought chaos and unemployment into his one remaining stronghold, and but for the timely aid of Federal relief agencies and work schemes, destitution and starvation would have wrought havoc among the millions who still dwell in the rural South. Leaders of his own race—Farm Demonstration Agents, teachers of agriculture in state and private colleges, Jeanes Supervisors—have for years been exhorting the rural Negro to grow more food in order to raise his standard of living, and unless in this great emergency he follows their advice and turns to a subsistence farming he will sink once again into that condition of complete dependence from which he was slowly emerging.

Yet the future, though uncertain, may surely be faced with hope and courage. The upward climb of the race has given it leaders of experience and wisdom who are able and willing to play their part in the difficult task of social and economic adjustment which lies ahead. Southern white folk, too, are learning to appreciate more justly the significance of the Negro in this strange new world. Organized labour, accustomed to look upon the Negro as a competitor, is realizing that it may be wiser to enlist him as an ally; Republicans and Democrats, as their social policies diverge, may even yet welcome his support. Southern women, the so-called "Hindenburg line of race relations," are learn-

---

[3] As waiters in hotels and restaurants, elevator operators, and as municipal employés engaged in street cleaning and garbage removal.

THE CHANGING SOUTH

ing the truth about their poorer neighbours, white and coloured; Southern churches, long bound by convention, are seeking to regain the truer freedom of the Christian gospel, and on Inter-racial Committees men and women of both races are coming to understand and respect each other as they work together for the community in which they live.[4] Above all, Southern youth, in high school and college, is asking questions and discussing social problems with a freedom from tradition, a realism, and an honesty which augur well for a future which is theirs to make or mar.

This new South of the twentieth century is in very truth a changing South. There are those who would hasten the change, and who look forward to a future in which North and South, town and country are blended into a homogeneous American civilization, planned, industrialized, progressive, modern. Others would prefer a slower development, and a South predominantly agricultural, continuing to make its distinctive contribution to a varied but none the less a national culture.[5] Both groups desire a more efficient school system, and all who have the welfare of the South and its people truly at heart realize that in any such future the Negro

[4] The outstanding example is the Commission on Inter-racial Co-operation organized in 1918 at Atlanta. Thirteen State Committees and several hundred local Committees in the South are affiliated with the Commission, and have assisted in arranging many Conferences and discussion groups. Other organizations such as Urban Leagues, Peace Committees and Community Chest Committees are also organized on inter-racial lines.

[5] Compare, for example, the discussion of Southern problems in W. T. Couch, ed., *Culture in the South*, and *I'll Take My Stand*, by Twelve Southerners.

must increasingly be allowed to play his part—not for reasons of prudence or sentiment but from "a conviction of justice, and loyalty to a consciousness of what is right." [6]

[6] From an address made by Dr. Dillard at the Peabody Conference, July 1930.

APPENDIX A

VIRGINIA RANDOLPH'S FIRST REPORT AS JEANES TEACHER

A Brief Report of the Manual Training Work done in the Colored Schools of Henrico County, Va. For Session, 1908–1909

Having taught Manual Training in Mountain Road School for sixteen sessions, I was recommended by the Supt. of Henrico Co. as Supervisor of the work for the entire county. My work began Oct. 26, 1908, under the auspices of the "Negro Rural School Fund" Dr. James H. Dillard of New Orleans, La. President. This work should begin in the primary grades and continue as long as the children remain in school. The destiny of our race depends, largely, upon the training the children receive in the schoolroom, and how careful we should be. The great majority of the children in the country schools will never reach a high school, therefore we must meet the demands of the schools in the Rural Districts by introducing this phase of training in every schoolroom.

It must be impressed upon the minds of the pupils that "Cleanliness is next to Godliness," and when this law of Hygiene is obeyed, they have conquered a great giant. They must also see that their schoolroom is neat and attractive with curtains at their windows, pictures on the walls, stoves kept neatly polished, and the grounds neat and clean, have a book on the "Laws of Health" hung in the schoolroom and each child be made to make himself familiar with it. The teacher should also give instructions along these lines

APPENDIX A

which will be of great benefit because the teachers are models for the school-room.

My first step was to organize School Improvement Leagues, the constitution says, that the grounds must be beautified and everything done to make an attractive school. Each scholar is expected to pay the sum of five cents per month and from time to time, give entertainments to strengthen the treasury but they must have a tendency to elevate the community morally and educationally.

During the term Mr. Wood gave me one thousand plants of hedge and twenty shade trees which I have distributed in each District. Hon. John Lamb of Washington, D. C., sent seeds for the school garden. Mr. Horace Peterson of Glen Allen, gave shucks to five schools for mats.

The schools are progressing nicely and with a few recommendations for next term, I will give a report from each school. I recommend:

I. The time given for Manual Training be six hours a week instead of three, and that time divided in periods to suit the teacher.

II. That the schools furnish their cooking materials and that the community may feel that they can order bread, cakes, etc. to be cooked at school and the proceeds made, go into the school treasury.

IMPROVEMENTS MADE AT EACH SCHOOL

BROOKLAND DISTRICT

Barton Heights School, Principal, Mary M. Scott

Fenced in the yard, granolithic walk, set out hedges, trees, and rosebushes, white washed the trees and fence, taught sewing, needlework, carpentry, and shuck mats. Amount collected during the term, $50.05, Expended, $10.95. Balance in the treasury for next term to fit up kitchen, $39.10.

Geter's School, Teacher, Mildred A. Cross

Enclosed the school with hedges, set out trees and flowers, taught sewing, making mats, and carpentry. Much interest

APPENDIX A 129

is being manifested in the school garden. Amount collected, $22.23, Expended, $6.63. Balance in treasury, $15.60.

Pole Road School, Principal, Emma J. Washington

Set out hedge, built a large pavilion, white washed the trees, planted flowers, taught domestic science, sewing, fancy work, laundry work, paper cutting, mats and carpentry. Much interest is being manifested in the school garden. Amount collected, $25.00, Expended, $10.00. Balance in treasury, $15.00.

Mountain Road School, Principal, Margaret L. Brooks

White washed trees, taught domestic science, sewing, and carpentry, kept the yard in good condition. Amount collected, $23.00, Expended, $12.63. Balance in treasury, $10.37.

Brookland School, Teacher, Lucy Wallace

Planted trees, flowers and hedge, taught sewing and paper cutting. Amount collected, $10.00, Expended $4,00. Balance in treasury, $6.00.

Coal Pitt School, Teacher, Beulah T. Harris

Taught sewing and paper cutting, could do no improvements on yard because property did not belong to the county. Amount collected, $5.00, Expended, $2.00. Balance in treasury, $3.00.

FAIRFIELD DISTRICT

Woodville School, Principal, Ernestine Christian

Set out hedge, white washed fence, planted trees, taught sewing, making mats, bead work and carpentry. Have a stove and cooking utensils ready for a kitchen. Amount collected, $7.85, Expended, $2.85. Balance in treasury, $5.00.

Benedict School, Teacher, Marion Steward

Taught sewing, making baskets, mats, boxes and carpentry. Amount collected, $3.02, Expended, $3.02. Balance in treasury, ———.

APPENDIX A

New Bridge School, Teacher, Racilia Steward

Taught sewing, making baskets, mats, boxes and carpentry. Amount collected, $8.38, Expended, $8.38. Balance in treasury, ———.

Boa Swamp School, Teacher, Annie M. Whiting

Planted trees and flowers, taught sewing and making baskets. Amount collected, $3.00, Expended, $1.00. Balance in treasury, $2.00.

Seven Pines School, Teacher, Corinne Stutely

Planted trees and hedge, built wood house, belfry,·bought a large bell. Amount collected, $10.35, Expended, $4.00. Balance in treasury, $6.35.

TUCKAHOE DISTRICT

Westwood School, Teacher, Virginia A. Taylor

Planted trees and flowers, white washed, taught sewing, shuck mats and carpentry. Amount collected, $12.00, Expended, $2.00. Balance in treasury, $10.00.

Green's School, Teacher, Pearl B. Rowe

Planted trees and flowers, taught sewing and needlework. Amount collected, $9.00, Expended, $6.00. Balance in treasury, $3.00.

Zion Town School, Teacher, Amanda Brown

Cleaned up an acre of ground and turned it into a lawn, taught domestic science, sewing and needlework. Much interest is being manifested in the school garden. Amount collected, $29.47, Expended, $16.69. Balance in treasury, $12.78.

Carbon Hill School, Teacher, Mabel V. Harris

Plowed up ground and made a twenty ft. walk, planted trees, rooted up stumps, taught domestic science and sewing.

APPENDIX A

Amount collected, $14.18, Expended, $4.00. Balance in treasury, $10.18.

Springfield School, Teacher, Bessie B. Langhorne

Planted trees, flowers and hedge, taught domestic science, sewing, and carpentry. Amount collected, $15.10, Expended, $3.10. Balance in treasury, $12.00.

Quioccasin School, Teacher, Mattie E. Tyler

Plowed up ground and made a thirty ft. walk, planted trees, set out hedges, put benches in the yard, taught domestic science, sewing and carpentry. Amount collected, $15.34, Expended, $3.00. Balance in treasury, $12.34

VARINA DISTRICT

Sydney School, Teacher, Martha Ross

The Chairman of Varina Board, Mr. S. C. Freeman, knowing how hard the teacher and patrons were working to build up their school, sent a good many workmen that he employed at Curls Neck Farm, to the school and fenced in the yard, put up belfry and bell, graveled the walk, built a porch, made benches and set out hedges; free of charge. He also assisted many of the other schools whenever called upon. Taught sewing and needlework. Amount collected, $5.30, Expended, $1.50. Balance in treasury, $3.80.

Bethel School, Principal, Estelle Ford

Made a ten ft. walk in front of school with flower borders, taught sewing and making shuck mats. Amount collected, $9.42, Expended, $1.91. Balance in treasury, $7.51.

St. James School, Teacher, Susie Monroe

Planted trees and flowers, taught sewing. Amount collected, $10.00, Expended, $1.05. Balance in treasury, $8.95.

APPENDIX A

Chatsworth School, Teacher, Blanche M. Kenny

Owing to the teaching in a rented place, could not do any planting, but taught agriculture in the school room, also taught sewing, and making baskets. Amount collected, $3.00, Expended, $1.10. Balance in treasury, $1.90.

Gravel Hill School, Principal, Mannie B. Jackson

Fenced in the school grounds, planted trees and flowers, taught domestic science, sewing and needlework. Amount collected, $40.80, Expended, $3.00. Balance in treasury, $37.80.

No. of schools, 22.
No. of visits during term, 190.
Amount collected, $331.49.
Amount expended, $108.81.

Balance in the different treas. to date for stoves and cooking utensils next term, $222.68.

I am indeed proud of the interest manifested by each teacher in carrying on the Manual Training work. Every school without any exception took hold of the work willingly and cheerfully, one can but admire the energetic efforts put forth by each teacher to carry out every suggestion that pertained to the advancement of the work. I hope by the beginning of next term, kitchens will be built in all the schools.

Respectfully submitted
Virginia Estelle Randolph

APPENDIX B

Reports by State Agents on Jeanes Work

Louisiana—Activities Engaged in by Jeanes Teachers
July 1, 1932, to February 28, 1933, inclusive
(Statements taken from reports of Jeanes Teachers)

Richland Parish
1. Canning of vegetables (July, Aug.)
2. Religious worship (July, Aug., Oct., Nov., Jan., Feb.)
3. Office work (July, Aug., Oct., Dec., Jan., Feb.)
4. Planning fall gardens (July)
5. Conducted teachers' conference (Oct., Dec., Jan., Feb.)
6. Visited patrons' homes (Oct., Dec.)
7. Classroom supervision (Oct., Nov., Dec., Jan., Feb.)
8. Conference with superintendent (Oct.)
9. Conducted teachers' institute (Oct., Nov., Feb.)
10. Conference with State Rosenwald Agent (Oct.)
11. Distribution of free textbooks (Oct.)
12. Planned landscaping (beautification) of school grounds (Oct.)
13. Red Cross work (Oct., Nov., Jan.)
14. Attended P.T.A. meeting (Oct., Nov., Jan., Feb.)
15. Working in interest of libraries in schools (Oct.)
16. Taught demonstration lessons for teachers (Nov., Dec.)
17. Attended extension course (Nov., Jan., Feb.)
18. Faculty meeting, Literary Club (Nov.)
19. Attended State teachers' association (Nov.)
20. Held conference with school board member (Nov.)

(Continued on p. 136)

Virginia—Summary of Work of 23 Supervising Industrial Teachers
Session 1912-13

County	Negro Schs. in county	Schs. visited regularly	Visits	Av. term in months	Schs. extending term	Extension in months	New bldgs. erected	Cost	Buildings enlarged	Cost	Buildings painted	Buildings whitewashed	Sanitary out-houses built	Schs. using individual drinking cups	Improvement Leagues	Money raised by Negroes
Albemarle	41	15	116	7	10	1	1	$350	..	..	4	6	2	10	21	$727.65
*Alexandria	5	5	25	10	..	1	..	..	..	..	1	1	1	5	5	400.00
Brunswick	43	14	98	6	40	1½	..	..	2	80	..	..	1	20	43	1,670.00
Buckingham	32	21	110	5⅝	2	1	..	..	1	34	1	6	2	21	14	537.73
Carolina	33	15	95	5	6	1	..	..	1	200	..	..	2	12	10	1,263.56
Charles City	13	10	132	5	9	1	1	600	2	280	..	7	2	10	13	532.12
Charlotte	20	6	26	6	3	1	2	280	1	90	2	2	4	4	6	1,333.50
Chesterfield	28	13	102	6½	1	1	..	..	..	..	4	8	4	13	19	716.53
Cumberland	20	16	16	5¾	16	1	..	1,000	..	..	1	12	6	8	19	610.00
*Elizabeth City	8	8	154	7	3	1	..	..	..	..	8	5	2	7	8	673.07
Fairfax	21	21	87	7½	..	1-2	..	..	..	..	..	..	..	..	13	341.00
Gloucester	31	26	240	6	27	1	1	5,500	..	..	1	4	14	24	31	994.00
Goochland	21	15	108	5⅝	8	1	..	..	..	..	..	..	3	15	15	298.50
*Henrico	23	23	250	8⅓	4	1	2	5,000	..	..	4	6	3	23	23	3,740.22
*Isle of Wight	14	10	68	5	6	3	..	..	..	..	1	..	1	1	6	1,325.32
Lunenburg	28	28	91	4½	6	1	1	300	3	200	1	..	28	28	19	1,200.71
Mecklenburg	45	35	149	5	4	1	1	1,100	..	..	1	3	7	5	45	924.50
Nansemond	35	20	102	5	5	1	..	..	..	..	2	..	..	10	20	453.28
Northampton	23	23	140	5½	16	1½	..	700	1	200	..	5	3	10	14	1,008.42
Nottoway	23	20	112	6	2	1	3	428	1	900	4	8	5	20	12	1,186.86
*Prince Edward	41	40	120	6	14	1½	2	1,550	..	50	6	5	10	40	40	1,365.00
Rockingham	8	8	220	7	3	1	1	..	..	..	..	..	..	6	3	316.00
Sussex	21	18	215	5	1	1	1	1,000	2	178	3	1	2	21	23	834.77
†Warwick	10	2	} 77	6	3	1	3	6,000	..	..	3	..	..	4	6	203.06
†York	14	5														
TOTALS	601	417	2,853	6	189	1	20	$23,808	15	$2,212	46	81	102	317	428	$22,655.80

* Same teacher   † Same teacher

Louisiana—Summary of Jeanes Teachers Reports*
July 1, 1932 to February 28, 1933, inclusive

Parish	Months worked by Jeanes Teacher	Visits to schools	Visits with teachers	Conferences	Visits to homes	Days in field	Money raised
Ascension	6	85	111	8	10	85	$ 245.57
Bossier	6	75	209	13	60	99	70.00
Catahoula	6	89	92	13	52	120	356.51
Claiborne	8	156	294	11	147	158	298.07
Concordia	5	68	134	28	213	71	109.66
E. Baton Rouge	6	68	118	20	128	51	253.00
E. Feliciana	6	68	123	32	45	110	324.29
Franklin	6	187	216	20	273	112	53.00
Lincoln	8	135	184	28	72	134	233.84
Ouachita	6	161	325	25	54	119	672.86
Richland	7	107	226	24	71	140	149.65
Sabine	7	150	188	28	236	103	667.30
Tensas	8	98	127	4	3	122	20.00
Webster	8	112	114	25	79	123	523.89
W. Baton Rouge	6	33	43	2	32	126	46.03
W. Feliciana	6	57	55	5	42	83	8.00
Totals	—	1,649	2,559	286	1,517	1,756	$4,031.67

*The above statistical statement is based on summaries for each paris h compiled from the monthly reports of Jeanes Teachers to the State Agent. These summaries show the varied activities of Jeanes Teachers, and copies of the summaries for two parishes are printed below.

APPENDIX B

21. Directed industrial work (Nov.)
22. Canning with home demonstration agent (Dec.)
23. Talked to parents (Dec.)
24. Attended Jeanes conference (Dec.)
25. Worked with Red Cross and P.T.A. in furnishing hot lunches for pupils (Dec.)
26. Conducted State testing program (Jan.)
27. Visited schools with State Agent of Schools for Negroes (Jan.)
28. Mimeographed material for Negro History Week (Jan.)
29. Checked free health material for libraries (Jan.)
30. Conducted child health campaign (Oct., Nov., Dec., Jan.)
31. Conducted home gardens campaign (Jan.)
32. Collected money for lengthening school term (Jan.)
33. Gave health talks (Feb.)
34. Started movement to lengthen all school terms (Feb.)

Franklin Parish
1. Conference with superintendent relative to year's work, appointment of teachers, etc. (Sept., Oct., Jan.)
2. Made community school survey; met the people (Sept.)
3. Organized P.T.A. and attended meetings (Sept., Oct., Dec., Feb.)
4. Made inventory and arranged free textbooks (Sept.)
5. Made plans for year's work (Sept.)
6. Organized all year round garden club (Sept.)
7. Visited school, helped teachers with daily program, explained the State supervisory program (Sept.)
8. Lined up canning project (Sept.)
9. Collecting money for school purposes (Oct.)
10. Observed teaching, discussed lesson plans and assignments (Oct., Nov.)
11. Helped teachers with registration and classification of pupils (Oct.)
12. Distributed free textbooks (Oct.)
13. Held meeting of garden club (Oct.)

APPENDIX B

14. Organized teachers of the parish in extension classes from Southern University (Oct.)
15. Taught demonstration lessons (Oct., Nov., Dec.)
16. Gave school play to raise money (Oct.)
17. Correspondence with teachers (Oct., Feb.)
18. Conducted teacher's institute (Oct., Feb.)
19. Demonstrated how to use the pressure cooker in canning (Oct.)
20. Campaign to beautify school grounds (Oct.)
21. Explained and demonstrated the use of the reading charts (Nov., Dec.)
22. Distributed special bulletins to teachers (Nov.)
23. Attended State teachers' association (Nov.)

APPENDIX C

A TYPICAL COUNTY EXHIBIT (KING WILLIAM COUNTY, VIRGINIA)
DESCRIBED BY JACKSON DAVIS [1]

"The Jeanes Teachers early hit upon the idea of having a county-wide exhibit at some central point either at one of the large schools or in the county courthouse. In King William County, Virginia, I have attended several of these annual exhibits. The Jeanes Teacher directs the entire program and is in the background. Most of the children as well as their parents come for a day to the county training school, which is centrally located, bringing their luncheon and having a sort of picnic. Each school assembles an exhibit of the papers written, the handicrafts, and the interesting work in drawing or design. In the handicrafts there are usually samples of sewing, handmade garments, ax handles, baskets, chairs, tables, and other pieces of furniture. These exhibits are attractively arranged and the name of the school neatly printed on a card. They are then inspected and judged by a committee, and great interest is taken as the awards of ribbons are made.

"When the parents and friends are assembled, the older girls from the larger schools give an exhibit of their work in sewing. They wear dresses which they have made and go through drills on the platform. The audience is able to judge the skill, taste, and attractiveness of their work. A committee of judges also passes upon these exhibits and

[1] From manuscript copy of an address by Mr. Davis at an Inter-Territorial Jeanes Conference, Salisbury, Southern Rhodesia, May 27, 1935.

APPENDIX C

there is the keenest interest in the award of prizes. At the appropriate time, the boys and girls and men and women who have worked under the guidance of the special teachers of agriculture or the home and farm demonstration agents, assemble outside in their different clubs. Then they are arranged in order and march in procession about the school grounds carrying banners and placards indicating briefly the results of the work undertaken by each club. These tell very human and interesting stories. For example, a group of girls would be organized into a Poultry Club and a brief statement showing their results and profit would be given. There would also appear a special group of children who had not been late for school, or who had not missed a day and children who in the medical inspection were rated as five-point children, that is, children with no physical defects or with defects remedied. The procession finally enters the assembly hall and there are usually talks from visitors and reports from the various clubs of boys and girls, as well as parents. At frequent intervals they sing. I recall one melody which seemed to stir the audience deeply. It followed a brief report on what the county was doing to meet the depression. The refrain was: 'I'll never give my journey over 'till I reach my home.' In this country, the people own small farms and have little wealth, but have a comfortable living. They look forward eagerly to this meeting once a year. The Jeanes Teachers have conceived this method of promoting a sense of solidarity on the part of the people, and they make it an occasion for recognizing and honouring students and adults who have done successful work. No one could attend one of these meetings without being deeply moved. It is the Jeanes work at its best!"

APPENDIX D

Table I

Number and Distribution of Negroes in the U. S. A.*

	1910	1930
Total population of U. S.	91,972,266	122,775,046
Negro population of U. S.	9,827,763	11,891,143
Negroes in South	8,749,429	9,361,577
Negroes in rural South	6,894,972	6,395,000 †

* Except where otherwise stated, the figures given are from the *Negro Year Book, 1931-32.*

† *Recent Social Trends in the United States* (Report of the President's Research Committee on Social Trends, New York, 1933), p. 567.

Table II

Occupations of Negroes in the U. S. A.*

Negroes gainfully employed	*1910*	*1920* †
Agriculture	2,893,674	2,178,888
Manufactures and mechanical pursuits	692,506	960,039
Domestic and personal service	1,099,715	1,064,590
Trades and transport	425,043	540,451
Professions	68,898	80,183

* Except where otherwise stated, the figures given are from the *Negro Year Book, 1931-32.*

† The figures for 1930 will probably show that the Negro has lost ground in the more skilled occupations owing to increased competition from white workers. He has also suffered greatly from unemployment during the economic depression.

APPENDIX D

Table III

Negroes of School Age in 17 Southern States and the District of Columbia, and Their Enrolment in Schools in 1930 *

Negroes of school age 3,326,482
Number enrolled in public schools 2,289,389
Number enrolled in high school grades ...... 148,754 †
Number enrolled in college grades .... 19,371 ‡

* Except where otherwise stated, the figures given are from the *Negro Year Book, 1931-32*.
† E. E. Redcay, *County Training Schools and Public Secondary Education for Negroes in the South*, p. 99.
‡ *A Survey of Negro Higher Education* (*Journal of Negro Education*, Yearbook No. II, July, 1933), p. 264.

Table IV

Comparative Statistics for Public Schools in 14 Southern States, 1929-30 *

	Enrolment in Negro public schools	Length of Term in days		Current Annual Expenditure per pupil		Wealth per capita of total population
		Negro	White	Negro	White	
Alabama ..	194,713	127	158	$10.09	$36.43	$1,284
Arkansas ..	110,853	132	150	13.02	38.15	1,447
Florida ...	90,108	124	163	14.45	57.16	2,046
Georgia ...	246,019	137	154	6.38	35.42	1,380
Kentucky ..	47,308	...	...	...	...	1,559
Louisiana ..	153,661	114	173	16.54	67.47	1,973
Maryland ..	51,690	178	189	43.16	64.86	2,705
Mississippi .	290,246	112	162	5.45	45.34	1,376
N. Carolina	260,135	138	154	15.71	40.07	1,837
Oklahoma..	48,384	142	150	34.25	43.86	1,756
S. Carolina	217,809	116	172	7.84	60.06	1,475
Tennessee..	115,219	149	167	...	...	1,970
Texas......	203,740	130	157	16.02	38.76	1,986
Virginia ...	152,622	142	165	...	...	2,189
Total ...	2,182,507	...	...	...	...	...
Average		134	165	$12.57	$44.31	$1,785
U. S. Average	...	...	...	$87.22		$3,088

* Fred. McCuistion, *Financing Schools in the South*, Tables IV and VII.

APPENDIX D

Table V

Summary of Income and Expenditures of the Negro Rural School Fund, Inc., 1907–1932 *

Income

From Fund Investments .... $	—	$1,036,467
From Contributions:		
Phelps-Stokes Fund	10,000	
General Education Board	1,087,194	
Rosenwald Fund	9,303	
Miscellaneous Sources	9,140	
Total from Contributions		1,115,637
		$2,152,104

Expenditures

Administration .... $	321,122
Salaries of Jeanes Teachers	1,670,848
Extension Work	51,093
Buildings and Equipment	20,781
Conferences	41,807
Summer Schools	10,819
Miscellaneous	5,109
	$2,121,579

* Arthur D. Wright, *The Negro Rural School Fund, Inc.* The Financial Tables in this volume give details for each year.

APPENDIX D

Table VI

Amounts Contributed for Salaries of Jeanes Teachers in Certain Years by the Jeanes Fund and from Public School Funds *

Year	No. of Teachers	From Jeanes Fund	From Public School Funds
1909	65	$ 14,759	---
1910	129	43,779	---
1912	109	36,140	---
1914	118	33,952 (84%)	$ 6,255 (16%)
1917	198	38,092 (62%)	23,692 (38%)
1922	275	101,282 (47%)	114,321 (53%)
1927	291	108,516 (40%)	164,871 (60%)
1932	320	88,264 (34%)	173,411 (66%)

* Arthur D. Wright, *The Negro Rural School Fund, Inc.,* gives the expenditure on salaries for each year from 1909 to 1932.

SELECTED BIBLIOGRAPHY

Much of the material for this study has been obtained by personal enquiry and from unpublished reports, letters, and other manuscript sources, as indicated in footnotes. Of the published sources, the following are the most important and accessible.

Brawley, Benjamin, *Doctor Dillard of the Jeanes Fund,* New York and Chicago, 1930.
Couch, W. T., ed., *Culture in the South,* Chapel Hill, North Carolina, 1934.
Embree, Edwin R., *Brown America,* New York, 1931.
——, ed., *Julius Rosenwald Fund: Review for the Two-Year Period,* Chicago, 1933.
Foreman, Clark, *Environmental Factors in Negro Elementary Education,* New York, 1932.
General Education Board: An Account of Its Activities, 1902–1914, New York, 1915.
Hendrick, Burton J., *The Life and Letters of Walter H. Page,* 3 vols., Garden City, N. Y., 1922–25.
I'll Take My Stand: The South and the Agrarian Tradition, by Twelve Southerners, New York and London, 1930.
John F. Slater Fund, *Occasional Papers,* especially:
 No. 27—*Selected Writings of James Hardy Dillard.*
 No. 28—W. W. Alexander, *The Slater and Jeanes Funds: An Educator's Approach to a Difficult Social Problem.*
 No. 29—Edward E. Redcay, *County Training Schools and Public Secondary Education for Negroes in the South.*

Jones, Lance G. E., *Negro Schools in the Southern States*, Oxford, 1928.
Journal of Negro Education, especially the following Yearbook Numbers:
   No. I, July, 1932, *A Critical Survey of the Negro Elementary School*.
   No. II, July, 1933, *A Survey of Negro Higher Education*.
   No. V, July, 1936, *The Reorganization and Redirection of Negro Education*.
Leavell, U. W., *Philanthropy in Negro Education*, Nashville, Tennessee, 1930.
McCuistion, Fred., *Financing Schools in the South*. Issued by State Directors of Educational Research in the Southern States as a part of the Proceedings of the Conference held at Peabody College, December 5 and 6, 1930.
———, *The South's Negro Teaching Force*, Nashville, Tennessee, 1931. Pamphlet.
Mims, Edwin, *The Advancing South*, Garden City, N. Y., 1926.
Murphy, Edgar Gardner, *The Basis of Ascendancy*, New York and London, 1907.
———, *The Present South*, New York, 1904.
Negro Year Book, 1931–32. Monroe N. Work, ed.; published at Tuskegee Institute, Alabama.
Peabody, Francis G., ed., *Education for Life: The Story of Hampton Institute*, Garden City, N. Y., 1919.
Washington, Booker T., *Up from Slavery: An Autobiography*, Garden City, N. Y., 1927.
Woodson, Carter G., *The Rural Negro*, Washington, 1930.
Wright, Arthur D., *The Negro Rural School Fund, Inc.* (Anna T. Jeanes Foundation), Washington, 1933.

www.ingramcontent.com/pod-product-compliance
Lightning Source LLC
Chambersburg PA
CBHW030111010526
44116CB00005B/200